# Who Am I That I Should Go?

# A Guide to
# Short-Term Missions

## Joyce Good Henderson

Faith's Loom Books

Who Am I That I Should Go?
A Guide to Short-term Missions

Copyright © 2012 by Joyce Good Henderson

Scripture quotations are from the *New International Version of the Bible*.

Faith's Loom Books

ISBN-13: 978-0615585987 (Faith's Loom Books)

ISBN-10: 0615585981

Published in the United States of America

## Acknowledgments

The Bible is full of ordinary people, like you and me, asked by God to do something more.  One of them, an old man, a fugitive from justice, a simple shepherd with a speech impediment, when asked by God to go to Pharaoh and free God's people answered:

*Who am I that I should go?*

My thanks to those who have provided me with answers to Moses' question:

Mary Hermiz, Sherrill Corson, Yolanda Cassidy, Roberto and Monica Contreras, Edwin Contreras, Cecilia de Cobo, Nanny de Cobo, Ken and Sarah Corson, Stan Doerr, Phil Henderson, Cindy Heyne, and Nate Paulk.

## Dedication:

## To Phil,

As I wrote this book, I agonized about trying to explain the reasons someone should become involved in missions. I knew the reason for myself, but I struggled to find the words to express my deepest feelings about my response to God's pull on my heart. It made perfect sense to me and for me but what about for others?

I finally asked my husband, "Why do you participate in Missions?"

I thought he would answer something like, "To keep you out of trouble."

But instead, his answer was simple, yet profound. "It pleases God—it's the right thing to do."

Thank you for your encouragement, support and willingness to keep me out of trouble.

# Contents

## Forward

# Forward

You have been thinking about participating in, coerced to go, or feeling called to go on a mission trip. Why? Because, as followers of Jesus Christ, it is what we all should be doing as a fulfillment of the Great Commission to *"go ye therefore."* Right. But what do we DO when we arrive at wherever "therefore" takes us? That is the question we all should be asking ourselves. What better answer do we have than to look first at the person who gave us this command and provided for us a model for mission wherever our mission experience takes us?

Let's look at such a mission trip in the Gospel of John—Jesus' encounter with the Samaritan woman at the well found in the Gospel of John, Chapter 4. This is a story of a well where a Samaritan woman went to draw physical water but received the gift of living water from Jesus. First, however, take a closer look at John 4:4 *"But He (Jesus) HAD to go through Samaria."*

There was a much preferred route for Jews traveling from Judea to Galilee. Samaria was not welcoming to the Jews. Although the route was much longer, Jews would avoid passing through Samaria due to political contention and vast cross-cultural issues. But Jesus HAD to go.

Jesus, guided by the Holy Spirit, led his diverse mission team (His disciples) directly into Samaria to Jacob's well. He had a mission to accomplish. As do we. I am not by any means encouraging mission teams to travel into high security alert or politically unstable areas. I am only emphasizing Jesus' model in listening to and allowing himself to be guided into mission by the Holy Spirit.

Jesus HAD to go.
We HAVE to go

i

# Who Am I that I Should Go?

The Holy Spirit is directing, calling, inviting us to travel to the well and drink. A well where we might be arrogant enough to believe we are the ones delivering the living water. Surprisingly, we find ourselves receiving a drink of the living water offered by Christ in the experience of our mission trip. And we (and our faith) are never the same. We HAVE to go.

Once in Samaria, Jesus sends his disciples into town to get food and he sits down at the well to wait. Wait for whom? He waited for the Samaritan woman. Then in the distance he sees her. There she is traveling at midday in the hot sun to draw water. No easy task to carry a large pot. Jesus didn't run to help or carry her pot. He waited.

I wonder what we would have done had we been the ones waiting at the well? I believe most of us as a mission team would have instantly jumped up and made every attempt to solve her every problem – carry the pot, give her toiletries, build her a house, take her temperature, her blood pressure, offer her candy!

No, Jesus waited. Jesus met her when she arrived at the well. Jesus was all about relationships. He carried nothing with him. He had nothing to offer the woman but himself. Jesus waited.

The most important and most critical component of any mission team is to focus on relationship building. As a coordinator and guide for mission teams for nine years, I often heard the mission team "receivers" exclaim, "Oh, yes, the team built a beautiful school, saw 200 patients at the clinic but, sister, we wished they had taken time to know US better."

What IF there were no project and we were simply called to go and wait and "meet" persons of another culture?

What a richness we as a mission team discover if we maintain this as a team objective and the project a secondary objective. We should travel as if we have nothing in our pockets or our suitcases to give. Just offer nothing more than ourselves first. The team project second.

At the well, Jesus looks directly into the eyes of a woman who has had several husbands and is currently living with a man who is not her husband. She has quite a reputation in the village. This woman has been judged and, because of this judgment, she is going to the well by herself and not when the other women draw water early in the morning.

This woman then immediately judges herself when she tells Jesus "How is it that you, being a Jew, ask a drink from me, a Samaritan woman?"

The judged and the self-judged. Jesus never judged her. In Jesus, the Samaritan woman found a level playing field. She was in what Father Gregory Boyle, the founder of Homeboy Industries in Los Angeles, California, calls "God's Jurisdiction."

On a mission team we all have a tendency to take into another culture our perceptions of what is right, what is wrong, the way it "should" be or, in other words, our judgments of persons, cultural differences, cultural comforts (or cultural discomforts). Let unconditional, nonjudgmental love that embraces, comforts and consoles be our guide. An absolute must if any semblance of trust and relationship or "living water" is to be shared.

Father Gregory says, *"Close both eyes; see with the other one. Then, we are no longer saddled by the burden of our persistent judgments, our ceaseless withholding, our constant exclusion. Our sphere has widened, and we find ourselves, quite unexpectedly, in a new, expansive location, in a place of endless acceptance and infinite love. We've wandered into God's own 'jurisdiction.'"* [1]

---

[1] Tattoos on the Heart, Boyle, Free Press, New York, NY, 2010, p. 145

We find ourselves drinking deeply of the living water on our mission trip if we allow ourselves to "close both eyes and see with the other one.

Finally, after what I determine to be a brief conversation between Jesus and the Samaritan woman, there is the exchange of water – the "living water." The Samaritan woman is so overwhelmed with the outpouring of love and compassion she has just received from Jesus she excitedly runs back to the village leaving her water pot at the well. This woman runs right back to the persons who have judged her and abused her to invite them to:

*"Come, see a Man who told me all things that I ever did. Could this be the Christ?"*
John 4:29

John 4:39 tells us:

*"And many of the Samaritans of that city believed in Him because of the word of the woman who testified."*

What an absolute joy it is when both mission team and mission team recipients are able to express, in retrospect, excitement from the blending of cultures and the assurance that all have been in the presence of Christ – and that all have drunk richly of the living water offered by a generous God.

We ALL go to meet at the well. We ALL drink. The invitation is given to us ALL to "Come!

Take a good long drink from a fountain of water that will spring up into everlasting life." God's Kingdom is expanded. We come back – we share – they (the mission team recipients) remain – they share. And, perhaps, because of the excitement and energy of the mission team experience, many others will believe in Him.

And more will accept the invitation to *"Come!"*

Our purpose in mission is to serve as Christ and expand the Kingdom of God. I have known Joyce Henderson for more than ten years now and our relationship is wholly built around our shared passion for mission and mission team involvement. It was a privilege and honor to guide her in cross-cultural orientation and then watch her make the journey to the well as she embarked on her first mission team experience to Ecuador. She has learned to drink of the living water graciously, gently, and generously. And because of her, many others have been drawn to *"go ye therefore"* and many have believed in Him from the Christ they have seen in her.

Joyce has learned much along her journey of mission. This book contains much wisdom and practical guidelines to assist others to have an equally rich experience in seeking and ultimately drinking from the well of living water.

So...whether you are thinking about participating in, coerced to go, or feeling called to go on a mission trip...may this book help prepare you for your journey to the well. And may the journey keep you thirsty for more! Jesus HAD to go.

Rev. Sherrill Corson
Director of Development
Mission Milby Community Development Corporation

Who Am I that I Should Go?

# Chapter 1

## Serving God, Serving Others

*"I have said these things to you so that my joy may be in you,
and that your joy may be complete. This is my commandment,
that you love one another as I
have loved you."*
John 15: 11, 12 (NRSV)

When a 7.2 earthquake struck Haiti in January, 2010, the United States and many other countries responded by sending rescue, medical, relief and reconstruction teams. With very little preparation, thousands of people, most of them volunteers, left their jobs and homes to go and do what they could to provide immediate assistance.   Thousands more have continued to return in the ongoing effort to help the people of Haiti.

Emergency relief, construction and medical teams have also responded to natural disasters and famines in other countries around the world since then. Aside from natural disasters, more than two million other volunteers go on short-term missions every year.

A short-term team may involve a few hours, a single day, a week or up to six months, and crosses cultural, and sometimes, geographical boundaries.

1

The location and the task can vary broadly, but there is always one thread connecting every mission project: *people* — people who have needs, the most important one being the need to know and experience the love of God.

* * *

Five-year-old Emily explained that she knew all about joy. "Joy stands for Jesus, others and yourself," she said.

*Jesus, others, yourself,* the priorities of life, in the correct order. When you put your life into this order, joy fills you, clings to you, saturates you to overflowing. A three-ply cord is strong. A three-legged stool stands firm. The power of God's love lives in the trinity of Jesus, others, and yourself.

## My Story

"I would make a great missionary nurse," I told my pastor. My church had recently hosted Mary, a missionary nurse who inspired me and invited me to join her work at a hospital in Kenya.

The pastor readily agreed. "You would make a good missionary. Someday."

*Someday.* Not now. I was a single mother with five young children.

"Your first responsibility is to your children. If God wants you to be a missionary, the calling will still be there when the timing is right."

Of course, I wanted it then. But, recognizing that my pastor was right, I put my dreams of serving in Africa on hold. The seed of desire of going to the mission field never left me. It also didn't occur to me that the mission field might be closer than I thought.

## Involving the Family

I wanted to raise my children to have compassion for all people, and to acquire habits of giving to others. I decided to concentrate on activities we could do as a family, since, with children from four to thirteen years of age, getting through each day was challenge enough.

**Sharing and giving are not innate virtues in children; they must be modeled and taught by parents.**

So, we began to look for projects for the whole family. Being involved in something outside of our own household gave me opportunities to teach my children the values and behaviors I prized. We started with outreach programs sponsored by our church in our own community, and we found many ways to share God's love in practical service to others.

Of course, my children balked at times. Occasionally, doing something together as a family and making it fun was reward enough; other times, I resorted to the bribery of stopping for ice cream on the way home from some event. We began simply by participating in fund-raising walks for local mission organizations, and collecting clothing and food for a community sharing center.

The first year I proposed we would ring the Salvation Army bell for an hour during the Christmas season, they objected. They didn't want to be seen by anyone they knew in front of the mall. So, I took the "Saturday morning at 7:30" slot. None of their friends would be up at that hour. To make it fun, I challenged each child to take a fifteen-minute shift. Whoever had the greatest number of people stop to contribute would be the winner. Competition made the effort more fun. Within a few years, bell-ringing became a family tradition, and my children actually asked if we could sign up for more than one time slot.

We volunteered in a soup kitchen, baked and served thousands of cookies for migrant farmers' Christmas parties, and worked on a Habitat for Humanity house. With the church youth groups, the kids went on mission trips. Later, when they were in college, several of them spent summer breaks working on mission projects.

## A Mind for Missions

Throughout these years, I still thought becoming a career missionary was the only way to go into the world and make disciples. Mission work took place in Africa, Haiti, India, or some exotic, foreign cities with starving children and scary diseases. I did not realize that mission work could occur in my own city, county and state. I did not connect that the thousands of opportunities for service, now called "servant evangelism" – sharing Jesus Christ through actions as well as words - can actually be mission projects.

Although I took seriously the commandment to go and make disciples, I really didn't know how. All of my friends and associates belonged to churches. God had always been a constant part of my life and of the lives of everyone I knew. How could I meet people who had never heard of Jesus Christ, especially in my community where there was a church on every street corner?

And, the word "evangelism" sent shivers down my back. I couldn't imagine talking about Jesus Christ to a stranger. What could I say? How would I say it? My faith was a very private part of my life.

Then, Sherrill Corson, a minister who worked with short-term mission teams, came into our lives with a message that seemed to be especially for me. She held a glass of water, clean and clear from a nearby faucet. Her simple message: water is readily available here, but that's not true in much of the world. The Living Water is also something we take for granted, and yet, there are people throughout the world who have not heard the message of salvation and tasted the water Christ promises.

She challenged me to leave my comfort zone, middle-pew America and go into the world. Twenty years after Mary's invitation to Africa, the timing was now right. God renewed His call and an opportunity became available to go on a short-term mission trip. Before I knew it, I had moved from local to global projects.

My children, who are all now young adults with their own families, and I have participated in one-day projects in our own community, in a neighboring county and within our state. I have traveled to mission sites within this country, and I have gone across international borders. The location and the task can vary broadly, but there is always one thread connecting every project: *people* — people who have needs, the most important one being the need for Jesus Christ. Over the past 20 years, I have learned and continue to learn about why and how an ordinary person can fulfill the commandment to go into the world and make disciples.

## Getting Started

Like most people, you have work that needs to be done at your own home, and precious little time. You wonder how you can find time to work on another person's house, or to serve a meal to someone other than your own hungry kids. How could you put the needs of someone else before those of your family and yourself? Our culture emphasizes positive messages, achievement, success, and wealth; but what society preaches, and what the Bible says don't always match.

God will work in your heart, soul and life, as well as in the lives of those in need. When you begin to adjust your focus from "me" and "mine" to "God's," you open the door to His possibilities, and His blessings. He will supply the time, opportunity, ability and desire. God doesn't ask for ability, but availability, and it's easier to send and support than to "be" and to "do."

Jesus' "riches to rags" story offers the model of servant-hood. The example of Christ challenges you to commit to serving others as an act of obedience to God's purpose, and the answer to the command to go into the world and make disciples of all people.

You may want to supply the answers to problems, but mission activities require an attitude of learning and serving. As you open ourselves to God's work within, enabling you to reach out to others, you will begin to see people the way God sees them. You can let go of your perceptions of others and "their problems," and grow in respect for the rich diversity of His creation. Missions is all about serving God by serving others, sharing God's love, not just your own efforts, and sharing your faith and personal knowledge of God.

If you desire to serve God in new and exciting ways, consider the experience of a short-term mission. If you have a mind for missions and a heart for others, God gave you these gifts. Participating in mission projects is your response to the seed He planted in your heart. Your desire to serve God can come through a sudden push, or a slow-growing awareness nurtured for many years.

## Adjusting your focus

There are three different ways to participate in missions: going, sending and supporting. The roles are not exclusive and you may want to become involved in all three roles. When I realized I could not go to Africa, I decided to support my missionary friend Mary and committed to send a regular amount each month. My church sent mission teams for short-term mission projects each year, and we supported them by helping them raise funds, and by showing interest in their work.

Going might not seem possible to you, until you learn as I did, that going doesn't mean getting a passport and packing a bag. Going means following the lead of Moses who asked God, "Who am I that I should go?"

God simply needs for you to be available to Him. *Availability* has nothing to do with *ability*. Make yourself available to God and let Him take it from there. He may have a unique solution as He did for Moses' inability to speak before a crowd. Aaron, Moses' brother did the talking. God always equips you to do the job He has called you to do.

The Bible is filled with stories of imperfect people busy with their own lives when an encounter with God changed them and their path. Should you expect any less of God who wants to work in your life? All He needs and expects from you, and me, is an open heart and mind willing to serve God by serving others, share His love, not just your own efforts, and tell others about your faith and personal knowledge of God. Mission projects allow you to live Jesus' message of hope that comes from faith, and teach others to do that. God can and will use anyone—even you, when you make yourself available to Him.

**Missions involves ordinary people doing extraordinary things for God and His people**

## Stepping out in Faith

You might be afraid to try something new, especially in a cross-cultural setting, but God is the author of new beginnings. It often takes courage and a leap of faith to:

- Step out of your comfort zone;
- Go to a place across town or across the globe to a place you've never been and don't know anyone;
- Learn to say "hello" in a different language;
- Speak to strangers about your faith;
- Share your personal experiences with God.

Look for a project; don't depend on someone else to find or create something. Consider the model of Jesus who met the physical needs for food, comfort, and wellness of body and spirit in the people he encountered. You can begin with your own church and community.

- What programs or ministries does your church already have or support?

- What organizations provide assistance within your community?

- How might you and your family fit into already-existing programs or projects?

- What projects interest you?

## Typical Community-based Ministries and Programs

Providing comfort
>Organizations helping women during
>>at-risk pregnancies
>Ministries visiting the sick and homebound
>Hospice programs, and ministries to
>>persons with HIV/AIDS
>Grief support and bereavement counseling
>>programs

Providing shelter, clothing and physical needs
>Shelters for the homeless and families
>Habitat for Humanity
>Shelters for abused women and children
>Salvation Army
>Thrift stores, projects that offer clothing,
>>shoes or blankets

Providing food
>Soup kitchens and meals programs

        Food drives and pantries
        Hunger initiatives

Providing for wellness of body and spirit
        Church outreach programs
        Vacation Bible School, childcare and
           after-school programs
        Mentoring youth
        Literacy, tutoring and English as a second
           language (ESL) classes
        Disaster relief projects
        Volunteer training

Remember, you don't have to "go it" alone. God is working in your heart, but He may also be at work in others, and it's always easier to try something new with people you enjoy. Pull together a group that might include your family, some friends, members of a home study group, youth, or a church class.

If no one but you and your children show up, don't be discouraged. Many people would rather be observers than participants. Follow God's leading anyway. Then, do it again. As serving others becomes a habit, you will see a change in your life. When others notice that change, they will ask how they can become a part of what you have started.

## The Ministry of Presence

Participating in short-term missions involves two basic beliefs: God has a heart for all people; and, God chooses to work through people, as inefficient as we are, to fulfill His plan. God can and will use us to whatever degree we make ourselves available to Him.

On the first day of a mission project in Santo Domingo de los Colorados, Ecuador, Pastor Nolberto Vivas explained the "ministry of presence." The work project and the Vacation Bible School we planned were not as important as the presence of the members of the mission team.

9

"You speak to the people of Ecuador by sharing yourselves," he explained in Spanish. "Just being here demonstrates how much you care."

On a mission project, whether it is one-day in your own community, or a week on the other side of the world, you show that you want to understand and know the hearts of other people. You want to share their burdens. The ministry of your presence and your service bring God's love to others' lives in practical, tangible ways.

There are always easier and more efficient ways to complete a task. You can send money to a mission organization. You can hire local persons in a Third World country to complete a construction project. You can ship medications and supplies to a missionary doctor. You can stay at home, worship in your church, and sleep in your own bed. But you'll miss an opportunity of a lifetime. You'll miss what God has in mind for you. Growing can be a scary prospect, but is it safer or better not to?

## Will You Serve?

When you go on a Short-term mission teams-Term Mission, God asks, "Will you serve me? No matter what the task, will you serve my people?"

During a visit with my then three-year-old granddaughter said, "I can go potty all by myself, but you can come with me and wipe my bottom."

I raised five children and have wiped many a bottom, but her invitation made the opportunity a precious gift. She wanted my presence when she could easily manage for herself. I could have dismissed her. I could have been insulted by her request. But I was honored. It was a privilege because of who was doing the asking.

Serving may not be glamorous, fun, easy or rewarding, but when you put others' needs ahead of your own, you make a powerful statement about faith, and you create opportunities for growth in yourself and those you serve.

*What good is it, my brothers, if a man claims to have faith but has no deeds? Can such faith save him? Suppose a brother or sister is without clothes and daily food. If one of you say to him, "Go, I wish you well; keep warm and well fed," but does nothing about his physical needs, what good is it? In the same way, faith by itself, if it is not accompanied by action, is dead.*
James 2: 14-17

When God calls you to do something, faith changes your answer from, "Who am I that I should go to...?" to "Who am I that I should say 'No' to God?"

You have been given an invitation...from God...from someone like me, a short-term mission team leader.  How will you respond?

* * *

*You first receive the dream by faith.*
*Then it becomes reality.*
*Each day must count for the dream.*
*Be faithful in the small things that work*
*toward the dream.*
Esperance Espy Ibuka,
missionary from Rwanda

## Action Plan

### Personal response:
God has concern for the whole world and wants you to share that concern. How can you develop a heart for God and for others that becomes a way of life?

### Awareness:
Anyone can help someone and feel good about the effort. That is not the reason to participate in a mission project.
How can you develop an understanding of God's heart for all people and how He works through you to fulfill His plan?

### Making a Difference:
List the talents and abilities you can make available to God.

# Who Am I that I Should Go?

# Chapter 2

## Go, Send or Get into the Way

*"Everyone can be great because everyone can serve. You
don't have to have a college degree to serve...
You only need a heart full of grace...
a soul generated by love."*
Martin Luther King, Jr.

### Can you hold a baby?

At an informational meeting for the first mission team my
husband and I led, Nita approached with a question. "How old
do you have to be to go on a mission trip?" she asked.

We knew she really wanted to know if she was too old to join a
short-term mission team. My husband answered, "For this
project, you must be at least sixteen."

Her eyes twinkled as she said, "Well, I'm seventy-nine. What
can I do?"

Even though the project involved laying tile and pouring
concrete to create sidewalks at a jungle church camp in
Ecuador, we would also hold Vacation Bible School every
afternoon at a local church. We needed workers who could mix
cement as well as help with a child.

"Can you hold a baby?" we asked her.

Nita signed on for that team and served on teams of the following two years. Over the years, we have taken people of all ages and various medical conditions. One team member brought her sleep apnea machine, several have been diabetics. As long as they receive clearance from their physician and understand the rigors of the trip, whether it is to the tropics or high altitudes, we will accept them on the team.

## Why go?

People participate in mission projects for a variety of reasons. Perhaps you will see yourself in their answers, when asked why they are involved:

- I want to learn, grow and be challenged more than I could possibly give.
- I'm looking for Christ.
- I've traveled a lot and I've seen poverty and ignorance and the need for Christ.
- I'm looking forward to helping mothers and children.
- Children are close to my heart and since I am from a Third World country, I know what they don't get. I want to share my love for Jesus Christ with them.
- I want to contribute and help them out.
- I want to see what I can offer to someone else learning about God.
- It's something I've always wanted to do, to see if I can help someone.
- To learn about the people and their way of life.
- I never understood what 'Third World means.
- I want a chance to see how others live, and learn about their culture.
- To share the love of Christ with others. I know you get more out of it than you give.
- God has called me to do this.

- I'm looking for a significant spiritual experience to break through to my heart.
- I want to share the love of Christ with others.
- I want to see people come to know Christ as their Savior and participate in missions.
- I hope to show through my actions my love for people and the Lord.
- I want personal interaction with the people to share my life experiences with them.
- It's the right thing to do. It pleases God.

---

The Four Basic Reasons for Participating:

- Jesus commanded it (Matt 28:19-20).
- All people need God's love, expressed in practical and spiritual ways.
- Our purpose as humans is to love God and serve others.
- Our desire to know God and follow Him can be met by participating in a mission project.

---

## What is a Short-Term Mission?

- A short-term mission (STM) is an opportunity for a person who is not a career missionary to participate in an experience that shares God's love in practical ways. The length of time can vary; a short-term mission may be a few hours, a single day, a week, or up to six months.

- A short-term mission (STM) crosses *cultural* and sometimes geographic barriers although the location may be nearby within your own or a neighboring community, or, at some distance, in your state, across the country or outside your country.

- A short-term mission is not about <u>where</u> the project is, but <u>who</u> you are called to be, and <u>what</u> you are called to accomplish.

- A short-term mission serves God by serving others, sharing His love, not just your efforts, and demonstrates your faith and personal knowledge of God.

A model for missions can be found in the early years of the Christian community. Some were called to go into the world. Others sent and supported them with prayer and finances.

*You will receive power when the Holy Spirit comes on you; and you will be my witnesses in Jerusalem, and in all Judea and Samaria, and to the ends of the earth.*
Acts 1:8

*After they (the disciples) had fasted and prayed, they placed their hands on them and sent them off.*
Acts 13:3

*When Lydia and the members of her household were baptized, she invited us to her home "If you consider me a believer in the Lord," she said, "come and stay at my house." And she persuaded us.*
Acts 16:15

## Going

Someone who **goes** shares God's love within the framework of another culture, whether it is next-door or across the globe. This person, a spiritual beginner or a mature believer, wants to help others in practical ways that often produce opportunities to learn more about Jesus Christ.

## Identifying a Go-er

1. Are you flexible and willing to learn?
2. Do you readily adapt to new and different environments?
3. Are you a risk-taker?
4. Do you want to serve God "in the real world?"
5. Do you believe that all persons are made in the image of God and loved equally by Him?
6. Do you ask: "Where is God leading me? What are the needs? How can God use me to meet those needs? How can I share the experience with others?"

# Senders

Those who go also rely on those who **send**. Senders are often a church, or organization that commissions and sends a short-term mission team. Senders coordinate resources to support those who go, assisting with fund-raising, collecting supplies, arranging transportation, and coordinating logistics for the project. This "rear echelon" role is very diverse, depending on the needs of the Go-er and the project.

## Identifying a Sender

1. Do you desire to serve "behind the scenes?"
2. Can you organize resources, raise funds, see the big picture, but work on the small details?
3. Are you an encouraging person who can support the team and its leader throughout the planning and implementation of the project?
4. Can you identify needs, mobilize and network with others to meet those needs?
5. Can you communicate needs to others and inspire them to participate as Senders?

Senders may also be an organization devoted solely to mission work. Frequently, such groups concentrate on one aspect of ministry, such as Habitat for Humanity working to provide affordable shelter for people throughout the world, or MAP International, dedicated to health care by supplying medications and promoting community health education and development.

## Prayer and Financial Support

The dictionary offers these definitions: support includes sustenance, provision, financial assistance, backing, maintenance, strengthening, confirmation, or bearing witness. Add "prayer" to this list. Those who **support** missionaries do more than give money (although that is very important and necessary). Go-ers need supporters who will pray for their safety, health, well-being and work. Every mission effort requires an under-girding of prayer.

Are you someone who can offer support by providing materials, resources, prayer and encouragement? We have had hundreds of supporters, most of whom we've never met. They sew lap quilts, crochet baby caps and booties, donate reading glasses, give clothing, buy diaper lotion, toys and school supplies for our teams. A box placed in a doctor's office came back to us filled with crayons, coloring books, baby vitamins and medicines. An anonymous person sent several dozen hand-crocheted baby caps.

### Identifying a Supporter

1. Do you believe God empowers all believers with opportunities for ministry?
2. When you get a raise or come into unexpected financial gain, do you ask God how you might be a resource for someone else?
3. Do you routinely pray for family, friends and your church?
4. Can you identify and collect resources for others engaged in missions?
5. Do you see the big picture as well as the details?

6.  Do you support others with finances, prayer and encouragement?
7.  How do you bear witness to the mission work of others?

Every believer has a role in missions, in fulfilling the commandment to go into the world and make disciples. You may be a Go-er, Sender, or Supporter, or some combination of these.

The church was not founded as an organization with one committee dedicated to missions. The primary purpose of **every** church, and every Christian, was and still is, making disciples. God's method for working in the world is to use people—ordinary people like you and me. God can and will use you to whatever degree you make yourself available to Him. Making a commitment to God gives Him a blank check on your life.

## Excuses, Excuses

Is there anyone whom God cannot or will not use for His purposes? Moses apparently thought he was one man God couldn't possibly use. God said to him, "So now, go. I am sending you to Pharaoh to bring my people, the Israelites out of Egypt."

Moses answered, "*Who am I that I should go* to Pharaoh and bring the Israelites out of Egypt?"

Moses continued to argue, complain and whine in spite of several miracles that would have convinced anyone it was truly God asking him to confront Pharaoh.

Jonah didn't even ask questions. When God told him to do something, he caught the nearest boat out of town. The Bible is full of whiners, losers, cowards, failures, but God turned them into heroes of faith. His method for working in the world is through people like you (and me). But only if you make yourself available.

## "I only have so much time."

Many people use vacation time, or occasionally someone may take a personal leave from work to go on a short-term mission. I can promise you that the mission experience will have a greater impact than any vacation trip, probably be less expensive than a week at a theme park, and give you greater energy to return to your daily routine. A mission trip is a great opportunity to get away and de-stress. Co-workers won't call and bother you. You'll be doing something so different, that you won't even think about your job. You won't even have time to worry about what awaits your return.

## "I'm too busy."

You can always make room in your schedule for an activity that captures your passion. A short-term mission project may also change your perspective on what is important in your life.

## "Missions isn't 'my thing.'"

Maybe not. But it is "God's thing." The church was not established as an organization with mission outreach as one goal. The church exists to spread the Gospel; the Gospel does not exist to spread the church.

A Christian's primary purpose is sharing God's love by serving others without regard to where they live or what language they speak. Obviously, not every person can go on a short-term mission team, but you can support mission activities. You can pray for missionaries, "adopt" a child through an international organization such as World Vision or Compassion International, contribute financial support or collect supplies for mission endeavors.

## "You have to sleep on the ground in the jungle."

Not necessarily. Mission projects take place in metropolitan areas, rural communities; in buildings, homes and churches; on mountains, islands; in jungles, deserts; and in your own community. You may work from home. You may stay in a hotel, travel by bus, eat excellent food and drink bottled water. Or you may sleep on a cot draped with mosquito net. Every project has different requirements. Choose one that matches your own needs and interests, or select one that may teach you new skills. The only "roughing it" might be an occasional power outage and a cold shower.

## "I don't have any skills."

Can you hold a baby? Can you do something that says, "I love you because God loves you?" Your presence is always more important that your abilities. A short-term mission experience is also a wonderful opportunity to learn something new.

## "It costs a lot to travel. I can't afford to go."

Then, get involved in a local mission. Many communities have a soup kitchen, thrift shop, Meals-on-Wheels, or Habit for Humanity office. Volunteer a few hours, then invite someone to join you.

Raising funds for a mission trip may seem impossible. Who will donate to the project? Are there Senders and Supporters in your life? Often your own family and friends will give to a mission project; you only have to let them know of the need. Many teams also conduct fund-raising events to assist with costs.

## "What about my kids?"

Take them with you. Teaching them to care for others requires you to model that behavior. Children are normally self-centered. Mission teams provide excellent support for learning to put others first, work as a cooperative member of something larger than self, and do something as a family. There are, of course, age limits for some mission projects, but many local efforts are family affairs.

## "I'm not a missionary."

You are a missionary. You are a person who can share God's love with another person by feeding a child, reading to a pre-schooler, painting a wall, mixing cement, washing dishes, serving a meal, teaching a class, measuring someone's height and weight, digging a hole, planting bushes, playing soccer. Actions always speak louder than words.

Words may not come easily. You may not be accustomed to sharing a personal story of how God is working in your life. That's okay. God will bless the time and effort you give to others. He will use you when you make yourself available to Him. Don't worry about winning souls, healing the sick, clothing the naked, etc. Pray that God will put you in the perfect place at the right time with the right words to make a difference. Be prepared for the chance that you may never know who or how you helped.

## "What about the needs here at home?"

As a nurse, I am very familiar with the concept of triage in which those with the most urgent needs receive priority in treatment. This doesn't mean the less severely-injured are ignored; they still receive treatment, but greater effort is applied where there is greater need.

In our country, we are blessed with social programs to provide assistance to the young, the impoverished and the elderly. Medical care is readily available for most people. Education is mandatory into the teenaged years. Our water is clean; our homes are warm. We have churches, and the freedom to choose the one where we will worship.

Yes, we also have poor. We have people who cannot afford medical care, or fuel to heat their homes. We also have people who have not heard about Jesus Christ. There are needs here at home.

However, even the poorest areas in my community, or in most communities in the United States, are better than much of the Developing World. It isn't poverty that kills the spirit, but the hopelessness of a limited future. We have been raised with the tradition that each generation is better off than the previous one. We pull ourselves up by our bootstraps. Many people actually believe there is a verse in the Bible that says, "God helps those who help themselves."

For the Developing World, this is not true. They cannot help themselves or pull themselves up by bootstraps they do not have. Political oppression, war, diseases we never face here, and unbreakable cycles of poverty trap people from one generation to the next.

**We, in the United States, are a small voice in the wilderness mumbling the Good News to ourselves while millions wait for the message of God's love and salvation.**

We don't have the solutions to all problems, no matter how much wealth and knowledge we possess. What we can do, however, is work to alleviate the poverty and hopelessness of the spirit because we have the Spirit of God to share. God can change lives when we first change hearts.

## Transformers and the Transformed

A short-term mission makes a considerable impact on everyone involved—those who send, those who go, and those who welcome. Growing in your relationship with God happens when you make yourself available to Him. Transformation comes when you yield to His agenda, when you listen to Him, not to

your own inner voice, when you leave your comfort zone to share His love with the least of His people.
God will teach you to rely on His strength rather than your own. As you witness God at work in your life and others' lives, He will show you how to reach out with love to a needy world.

\* \* \*

*After they had talked it over, Peter got up*
*and spoke to them.*

*"Brothers," he said, "you know that some*
*time ago God chose me to take the good*
*news to those who aren't Jews. He wanted*
*them to hear the good news and believe.*
*God knows the human heart. By giving the*
*Holy Spirit to non-Jews, he showed that he*
*accepted them. He did the same for them*
*as he had done for us. He showed that there*
*is no difference between us and them.*
*He made their hearts pure because*
*of their faith."*
Acts 15:7-9

## Action Plan

### Personal response:
Examine your excuses. What is stopping you from answering God's call?

### Awareness:
Identify the skills you have to give toward changing someone else's life.

### Making a Difference:
Be that ordinary person doing something extraordinary for God and His people.

# Who Am I that I Should Go?

# Chapter 3

## Putting Yourself in the Picture

*Sometime ago, a missionary handed me several photos of mothers with babies, and children with huge brown eyes and rosy cheeks.*

*She said, "Pick one that you can relate to."*
*I did, then she instructed,*
*"Now put yourself in the photo."*

*I joined a short-term mission team to Ecuador.*

### Helping, Healing and Hope

When several of my children were teens, they came home from a shopping trip, and headed for the bedroom closets. I found them putting every spare blanket we had into the car.

"What's up?" I asked.

"There's a homeless man living behind the shopping center, and he's cold," they replied.

"Let's talk first," I suggested.

The kids had a noble intention to meet the physical needs of the man living behind K-Mart, but there was much to consider.

First, how can we reconcile our desire to improve a life with a way of giving that:

- is appropriate;
- preserves the self-esteem of the recipient;
- allows him to be a partner, rather than subordinate in the process; and
- demonstrates God's love by pointing him toward a relationship with Him?

\* \* \*

**Giving, in missions, goes beyond providing material goods. Giving needs to be accompanied by helping, healing and offering hope.**

**Helping** provides opportunities to share God's love in a way that affirms a person's dignity as a human. **Healing** invites the person to connect to God, and gives **hope** for the future.

God challenges each person to commit to serving others by giving all that we can *have* to all that we *know* Christ to be. Servanthood is an act of obedience to God's purpose, and the answer to Christ's command to go into the world and make disciples of all people. God's intention for us is to love one another and to be a witness for Christ by performing our ministry where we have been called to do it.

## Relief and Development

Good-hearted desires to make things right are sometimes the wrong way to approach a situation. Whenever possible, helping others to help themselves is a better goal. Relief provides materials and assistance during, and immediately after, an emergency or natural disaster. Meeting needs during an emergency is always appropriate. However, continuing to provide relief over a long period of time encourages dependency.

29

After a generation of feeding people in drought-stricken areas of Africa, aid workers are now realizing that farmers are not working the land, even though agricultural conditions have improved. They no longer know how to grow food for themselves.

Development, on the other hand, recognizes the worth of all people, encourages and empowers them to solve their own problems, and meet their own needs, perhaps with assistance, but always preserving their self-respect. Development helps others to *become* more rather than to *have* more. Development is a hand up rather than a hand out.

## Types of Mission Projects

Mission projects can be divided into two basic types, according to their goals: *relief* and *development.* Relief projects fill an immediate need, such as providing aid after a disaster, setting up a temporary medical clinic, establishing a shelter for people displaced by a hurricane or flood. When Jesus changed water into wine at the wedding feast, He offered a model for meeting immediate needs. Jesus' miracles of healing and feeding masses offered aid, with the intention of restoring faith in God and hope for a better future.

Short-term missions (STM) also focus on development, which concentrates on longer term needs, a hand-up rather than a hand-out. Development empowers people to identify and begin to meet their own needs. Construction projects often fall into this category. Establishing a permanent presence in a community through a church, school, orphanage or clinic are all development projects. Participatory development values others, enhances their self-respect, and gives them ownership of problem-solving.
Whether it is a relief or development project, *serving others* is always at the core of short-term missions.

> Basic Types of Projects
> 1. Construction
> 2. Medical/Healthcare
> 3. Education/Training
> 4. Evangelism/Church Planting

## Tying Rebar

Construction projects usually require some level of experience and aptitude, although not necessarily from all team members. Several persons should have some degree of knowledge and competence; everyone else simply needs to be flexible enough to learn a new skill. However, experience has taught us that what you expect to do is not always what you will do. Building projects are frequently staged over the course of several months and more than one mission team. Your work will depend on what the team(s) before you have accomplished. There are other variables as well, such as the weather, availability of materials and workers, tools and equipment, and accessibility to plumbers, electricians, engineers, master craftsmen.

Our first construction team was supposed to lay tile. We brought the appropriate tools and knee pads with us, but when we arrived, we discovered that the floors were not ready for the tile. We painted walls, mixed and poured The next year, we were ready to mix and pour concrete to add a third floor to a school. The support columns had not been completed by the previous team so we learned to cut and tie rebar, and once again, we painted walls.

The third year, we were to lay block to build the walls of a community center's third floor. Over the course of one week, twenty-four out of twenty-six team members had the flu.

31

The walls crept up slowly, and we also painted the first floor rooms. See a pattern here?  It doesn't matter if you don't know how to mix cement with a shovel, or if you can't climb up on a roof, you can paint walls.

Construction projects provide wonderful opportunities to do something you might not ever do at home, to learn new skills, to work alongside the people of the host culture, and to have some tangible results from your labors.

These endeavors can also be frustrating when plans go awry, when task becomes more important than building relationships, or when "things aren't done as we do them" or as we think they should be done.

If you want to go home tired and sore, but with photos of your accomplishments, choose a construction project. But always keep in mind that the task is not the most important part of a mission project. People are. Try to get to know someone from the work site. Even if you stumble with the language, smile and shake a hand. Ask if you can take a photo together as a remembrance (una recuerda, in Spanish). Get to know your team members better, as well. The walls will always need painting, but people come first.

## Needed for Construction Projects

1. Personal protective gear such as goggles, work gloves, steel-toed shoes or boots
2. Work clothes and a hat
3. Flexibility and a good sense of humor
4. Humility and a spirit of cooperation
5. Willingness to give ownership of the project to someone else
6. The ability to do it "their way" even when yours might be better, faster, cheaper

## Take Two and Call Me

A medical or healthcare short-term mission project is completely different from construction. Members of this team need to have specific skills and experience in healthcare; however, you don't have to be a doctor, dentist, nurse or pharmacist. Lay persons can do many jobs on a medical mission team. You can assist by filling out records, measuring patients' heights and weights, checking vital signs, conducting simple vision screening for reading glasses, filling pill bottles, or entertaining children. Don't forget, there's always a baby that needs to be held.

A medical mission project may not be the best fit for the task-oriented person. When the relationship is the task, the goal is to help people in ways that are practical and relevant to their needs.

## Needed for Medical/Healthcare Projects

1. Time management skills—there will always be more patients than you can possibly see in the allotted time
2. Triage skills—the ability to assess and direct treatment of patients with different needs
3. A spirit of caring & compassion
4. A holistic approach that integrates the physical, spiritual, and emotional aspects of life
5. Patience and listening skills
6. The ability to think outside the box and come up with novel solutions to common problems

## Teaching the Teacher

The education/training short-term mission can be the most difficult one because of the inherent challenges in crossing cultures. People have a natural tendency to resist when outsiders come in to "tell them how to do it." The very nature of a short-term mission does not usually allow time for the building of relationships that deepens rapport and respect. Hence, the teacher in a cross-cultural situation needs to be sensitive to the needs of the student, the method of presentation and the objectives of the lesson.

Linda and I went to a new pre-school to work with the mothers whose children would be attending the school, and with their teachers. We prefaced each meeting by introducing ourselves as mothers like them, with the same cares and concerns that every mother has no matter where she lives or what language she speaks. Because we shared information mother-to-mother rather than "expert" to student, the messages had greater effectiveness.

## Needed for Education/Training Project

1. Materials in the language and at the learning level of the target audience
2. Rapport and respect on both sides
3. Patience for the slow nature of change
4. The ability to accept others where they are and invite them to grow
5. The ability to see others as God sees them
6. The ability to do it "their way" even when yours might be better, faster, smarter

## Mustard Seeds

Evangelism/church planting mission projects sow the seeds Christ talked about. Some landed on questionable soil, others on rock, but a few on good soil where, when nurtured produced plants.

A Visiting Bible School (VBS) is an excellent opportunity to introduce Jesus to children and, second-hand, to their parents. We don't call it "*Vacation* Bible School" because usually, the kids are not on vacation, and neither are we. Vacations are a one or two-week break from your regular job for the purpose of relaxation or change-of-pace. Sharing the message of God's love and salvation should be a part of our day-to-day lives, not an activity relegated to spare time or breaks from real life.

Evangelism projects often blend the caring and compassion of a medical mission with the rapport-building aspect of an education project. This STM also encounters the same challenges of working within a cross-cultural setting.

## Needed for Evangelism/Church Planting Project

1. Willingness to immerse yourself in another culture
2. The desire to fulfill the Biblical command to tell everyone about Jesus, "in Jerusalem, in all of Judea, in Samaria, and everywhere else in the world"
3. The ability to create in others the desire to know more about Jesus Christ
4. Flexibility, courage, humor, and talent for juggling
5. The ability to share yourself and your faith with another person and culture
6. The ability to approach persons as brothers or sisters no matter what their culture, language, living condition or religious beliefs

## Typical Mission Jobs

This has been a brief overview of the types of projects you might find on the mission field. Within a short-term mission, there may be a combination of projects. Every time we have had a construction or medical mission, we have offered VBS, and often, some sort of adult education. In addition, on a STM, you might find a nurse shoveling cement, an engineer checking blood pressures, a physician demonstrating crafts, a dentist twisting balloons into animal shapes. What tasks could you perform from this list of typical mission jobs?

# Who Am I that I Should Go?

| Distribute water | Take photos | Read books to kids | Make Craft Projects |
|---|---|---|---|
| Bring school supplies | Deliver medicines | Do a Puppet show | Glue foam crafts |
| Bend & Cut rebar | Fill pill bottles | Give Devotions | Witness your faith |
| Sweep floors | Team first aid | Keep a team journal | Make hand-prints |
| Paint walls, ceilings | Change diapers | Translate | Play games |
| Install Wiring | Give injections | Teach CPR | Blow bubbles |
| Pass cement buckets | Hold a light for a dentist | Teach teeth brushing | Make housecalls |
| Dig trenches | Play soccer | Show videos | Cut out crafts |
| Conduct VBS | Fit glasses | Tell stories | Greet & hug |
| Wash faces and hands | Pass out vitamins | Make balloon animals | Lead a worship service |
| Dig a garden | Move furniture | Serve meals | Peel vegetables |
| Pound holes in block | Provide medical care | Help a sick teammate | Pack & unpack a bus |
| Screen Vision | Put lotion on cheeks | Tell Stories | Entertain kids |
| Mix Cement | Check vital signs | Help cook a meal | Hold Bible studies |
| Pour Concrete | Cut cantaloupe | Carry luggage | Pray with people |
| Pass concrete blocks | Dispense medications | Tie rebar | Put socks on children |
| Plant bushes | Split pills for | Sing | Plumbing |
| Haul gravel | Hold a baby | Feed children | Deliver clothing |
| Wash Tables | Weigh children | Color pictures | Dress a Baby |
| Collect/Dump trash | Comfort the sick | Clean a kitchen | Play music |
| Wash tables | Visit schools | Teach songs | Hold babies |

## Choosing a Project

Evaluate carefully as you look for a project that matches your availability, interests and skills. Ask yourself:
- Where do I want to go and what do I want to do?
- What projects or organizations does my church already support?
- Does my church have an affiliation with a national mission organization?

## Team Questions to Consider

1. What services, resources, in-country arrangements does the sponsoring organization provide? How closely does it work with local missionaries or church leaders? Who are the hosts?
2. Whose project is this? The organization's or the local hosts'?
3. What are your responsibilities/their responsibilities?
4. What training do they provide?
5. How many people will you need on the team, and what age groups?
6. Do your skills meet their needs?
7. Do the dates of the project meet your schedules?
8. What is the policy for last-minute cancellations?
9. How do you fit with the philosophy and values of the organization?
10. What insurance (travel and health) is available through the organization?
11. What is the cost per participant?
12. Can you get the job done, or does the project require more than one team?

There are hundreds of mission opportunities at home and abroad available through churches, organizations and listed on the Internet. According to *Mission Maker Magazine,* in 2005, 40,000 churches and organizations sent more than one million short-term missionaries into cross-cultural missions. *Servants in Faith and Technology* Executive Director, Tom Corson reported in 2008 that 2.2 million people participate in short-term missions every year. Most of those involve travel to another country, however, if mission projects at home work better for you, you can find them in every community.

* * *

*Jesus said, "What shall we say the kingdom of God*
*is like, or what parable shall we use to describe it?*
*It is like a mustard seed, which is the smallest seed*
*you plant in the ground. Yet when planted, it grows*
*and becomes the largest of all garden plants, with*
*such big branches that the birds of the air*
*can perch in its shade."*
Mark 4: 30-32

## Action Plan

### Personal response:
Choose the type of project that meets your interests, skills, abilities and talents. Then, ask God to confirm that's the one He wants you to do.

### Awareness:
How do you expect to be affected by a STM?

### Making a Difference:
Put yourself into the picture of a STM by listing the jobs you could do.
Investigate projects available in the community in which you live.

# Chapter 4

## Leading a Team

*For many people, the question may not be*
*what you will do on a STM, but who you'll do it with.*

As a team leader, your first job is to trust God's plan for you and your team. The STM team is a continuous exercise in aligning and re-aligning your priorities to God's purposes. Allowing Him to equip you for the task of leadership can bring you into a deeper relationship with Him and with others.

Step one: put aside your own agenda. This is your opportunity to ask, and perhaps receive answers to the questions:
- Who am I?
- Who is God?
- What personal and spiritual growth and change does He have in mind for me?

Leading a team is, without question, a challenge. Add a cross-cultural setting and you will be stretched in many new ways. Team members look to you to have it all together, to have immediate answers for their questions, perfect organization, and spiritual maturity. Please don't place these unrealistic expectations on yourself!

**Leading a STM is Holy Spirit work.**

When you are following God's plan, you can trust Him to work out the details, internal and external. Prayer along with preparation is the key.

## Leaving Mom at Home

Working in cross-cultural mission, whether in your own community, or across the globe, requires that you listen, ask questions, suspend judgment, and refrain from offering advice to fix others' problems, whether they are on your team or your hosts. Your goal, in missions, is to empower others to solve their own problems, whenever possible.

I call that leaving "mom" out of missions. As a mom (and nurse), my life revolves around solving others' problems. "Where's my backpack?" "What's for dinner?" "Can Kim spend the night?" "Can you take me to the library?" "Grace has a rash. What should I do?" "What should I do about the neighbor's child using bad language around my kids?"

A parent's role as problem-solver never ends. Except during a cross-cultural mission. In that setting, you may encounter situations in which you know the right answer, the infallible way to solve some problem. The challenge, then, is to help others find their own solutions, what works best for them in their lives. In doing so, you encourage others to own their problems and you empower people to solve them.

In mission settings, there can also be problems that tug at your heartstrings. You are there because you want to help people, and share God's love with them. However, you can become overwhelmed by the basic human needs confronting you. You may not know how to help. You can become discouraged and frustrated by your own inability to solve problems.

First, recognize you cannot solve all of the ills of the world. Even though you feel great sympathy, you must recognize your own limitations. The fact that you have made a decision to serve God in a setting outside your comfort zone is the single

41

most important step you can take toward helping others.

**Being there is more important than
doing something or fixing something.**

Others might not recognize that. They want you to solve their problems. When you don't have the answers, there will often be someone who does. There are two options in these situations. First, tell the person you don't have what they need, but you will try to direct them to someone who may be better equipped to help, and second, as the person if he would like for you to pray with him. If you are working at a center or program, or for an organization, refer to the director. Pastors can also provide more resources to help.

Many times, prayer is all you can offer, but prayer can bring great comfort when no other solution seems readily available.

## What's on Your STM To-Do List?

So, you've committed to go on a short-term mission, perhaps to lead a team, what's next?
- Get a passport and immunizations.
- Buy airplane tickets.
- Purchase Bible School supplies.
- Invite twelve of your closest friends to join you.

That's a start, but there's a lot more to leading a STM.

## A Leader's 3 Areas of Responsibility

1. Target
   - How will you decide where God is calling you to go?
   - Will the project be someplace in which you have some interest or inclination?
   - Will you go where the need is greatest?

- Is there a local missionary, an established relationship or a project already present in the location you are considering?

2. Task
    - What will be the day-to-day activities of the project?
    - What do you hope to accomplish?
    - Will there be opportunities to develop relationships and friendships with the hosts?
3. Team
    - What criteria will you set for selecting team members?
    - What will be the age/health requirements of the project?
    - What spiritual gifts or natural talents will be needed?
    - Who will you invite to join the team?
    - What is the cost of the project? What budget will you need?
    - What funds are available from resources other than team members?

**You can invite people, but only God twists arms.**

Six weeks before we were to leave for an all-women's medical mission team, a team member suddenly cancelled. With only 48 hours left before the deadline to fill the slot or lose an airplane ticket, I faced a dilemma. I had already invited everyone I knew, and even a few people I didn't know.

Then, Amy called. "God woke me up in the middle of the night and told me to go," she said.

I barely knew her, although we went to the same church. And, I had never heard such excitement in anyone's voice. "He did?" I asked.

"Out of a sound sleep. I waited until 9 a.m. to call you. What do I need to do to go?"

Still amazed, I quickly ran through the steps. "You'll need a passport, immunizations, physician's release, and application form. And, it all has to be done in two days."

The church had already set aside funds for the person who had cancelled, and Amy would be able to use them. Within forty-eight hours, she had applied for her passport, started the series of immunizations, completed the paperwork and scheduled an appointment with her physician.

That mission trip so profoundly affected her that when she came home, she applied to return to college for a nursing degree. Her experience motivated her husband to join a STM team to Appalachia, and her sister joined her on another team two years later.

## Timing

How much time will you need to put together a STM? Six to nine months is an ideal length of time for planning, especially if the project is in another part of the country or abroad. Obtaining passports and immunizations often require at least six months.

## Sample Timetable

Month 1   Presentation to church committees for approval and
              support
          Contact host organization
          Informational meeting for prospective team members
          Member applications and airline deposit due
          Members apply for Passports and start
              immunizations
          Establish a budget

Month 2    First team meeting to get acquainted
           Plan fund-raiser if needed

Month 3    Second meeting; second payment may be due
           Fund-raising event held

Month 4    Third meeting, third payment may be due
           Assign team jobs

Month 5    Fourth meeting; fourth payment may be due
           Begin collecting supplies, VBS materials

Month 6    Fifth meeting, final payment and all paperwork due

Month 7-8  Cross Cultural Training
           Packing party
           Commissioning or Send-Off Ceremony
           Trip
           De-briefing meeting after trip

The timetable is meant to be a suggestion, primarily for beginning leaders. Having led a dozen or more short-term mission teams, we have shortened the meeting timetable to about three months ahead of the trip. However, we do begin at least six months before a trip with a general informational meeting so that team members can start their fund-raising early enough. If the trip is an overseas one, you also need to build in extra time for members to get passports and immunizations. We also work cross-cultural training into every meeting now, rather than having one separate meeting for that purpose.

## Information, Please

Your church may require a presentation of the proposed short-term mission to a missions committee or administrative board as well as the general membership of the church. Offer an overview of the project, timetable and budget. Graphics, maps and photos help, if you have them. You may feel compelled to "sell the idea," however, keep in mind that you only need to plant the seeds for God's nurturing.

You may meet resistance. You need not apologize for passion about world missions unless you believe Jesus Christ made a mistake when He told us to go into the world, or He didn't really mean to save all people. There are always people who do not share your vision or your calling.  Peter experienced this when he preached to Gentiles.

> *"The apostles and the brothers throughout Judea heard
> that the Gentiles also had received the word of God.
> So when Peter went up to Jerusalem, the circumcised
> believers criticized him and said, 'You went into the
> house of uncircumcised men and ate with them.'"*
> Acts: 11: 1-2

The Bible is clear: we are called to make disciples in all parts of the world.  If you, like Peter, have been called by God, nothing more needs to be said to those who disagree.  No one can argue about a calling from God, especially if it wakens you from a sound sleep.

## Welcome Mat

You've sent invitations, word of mouth carried them even farther, and people are responding.  While I believe that all Christians are called by God to participate in some form of mission activity, not all persons are called to go on a short-term mission team.  You can and must set criteria for your team members.  Obviously, the project, location and travel requirements will set some of your guidelines.  As you develop your own set of criteria for your team, here are some considerations.

## Sample Criteria for Participation in a STM

- Does the person have any training, education, life experience, natural abilities or spiritual gifts that match the needs of the project and team?

- What are the individual's motives, personal agenda, or reason for involvement?

- What do others say about the person's ability to work on a team?

- Are there any major life issues or medical concerns that could interfere?

- Is the person flexible, willing to learn, to serve and to follow instructions?

- Does the person have sensitivity toward the beliefs, customs, daily life and religion of other cultures?

- Does the person have the ability to suspend a desire to "fix" something or someone?

## Consider Attitude

Attitude is the single most important factor in determining who might join a STM. The person with a mission's mindset:
- Desires to share the love of God with others, without regard to their location, culture, religion or lifestyle;
- Understands that God works through imperfect people to accomplish His perfect plan;
- Respects all religions, but firmly believes Jesus is the way, the truth and the life;
- Commits to being open to learning and serving.

## Age and Infirmity

Consider age and disability carefully, but don't rule out participants solely on either basis. Our teams have successfully included people in their 70's and 80's, diabetics, asthmatics, those who have had open-heart bypass surgery, or who must use special medical equipment. We require all participants to have a physician's written statement that they can handle the conditions of the trip, especially a change in altitude, food and water.

Special precautions must be taken if you include youth on a STM. Some organizations now require that every member of the team be fingerprinted and subjected to a background check if persons under eighteen are on the team. You might consider requiring a parent of the youth to be on the team if you accept youth.

Having a family on the team is an excellent opportunity to instill the virtues of team participation in children. One caution, when you have a family on the team, there are two leaders—you and the parent. You may want to talk with the parents and children about expectations, roles and responsibilities during the STM.

## Appearances Don't always Count

Ted had lived overseas most of his life, yet he had very little insight into and sensitivity toward other cultures. Of course, we didn't discover that until we were in another country and his behavior jeopardized both our team and the long-term missionary who was our host.

Another team member on a different team had kept secret her ability to speak a foreign language. This would have helped us a great deal in our planning had we known she could serve as a translator. After serving on two mission teams, one participant complained that "we prayed too much."

Team meetings prior to the trip are not just for conveying practical information to team members. Use this valuable time to evaluate the flexibility, willingness to serve and learn, and spiritual growth of your team. If a team member's behavior is slightly difficult to deal with in pre-trip meetings, it will be magnified under the pressure of the trip.

Consider how you will handle persons who could create problems. On a trip with a large number of youth, we told them that any problems would result in sending them home immediately, at their parent's expense. A couple of the kids did find a way around this warning. They waited until the last night of the trip. We wished we had added the threat of never taking them on another trip.

## Long-Term Impact

Be open to change in your life, in the lives of your team members, and in your church. Once you have been on a STM, you might never be the same again. You may see your world, your life, your home, your church and your work differently. You may experience a desire to serve God in new ways, perhaps with newly-acquired skills, and with a more global perspective.

You may witness God at work in your life and others' lives. On a recent project, we repeatedly experienced the feeling of being in the right place at the right time. We saw God at work nearly everyday in the lives of the people and of our team.

\* \* \*

## Changed Lives

On our first trip to Cayambe, Ecuador, I noticed a woman washing clothes at the cement sink outside her home next to the church, site of our construction project. I asked our interpreter if we might go over and speak with her. The interpreter agreed, but told me the woman did not attend the church. I shrugged and continued walking toward the house.

I introduced myself and shared photos of my family, then, asked the woman about hers. She had a child who was seven years old and just beginning to walk. When I looked puzzled, she motioned him to come closer. Pulling up his pant leg, she showed me the scars on his leg. He had fallen into a fire as a baby and suffered severe burns. The scars made it difficult and painful to walk.

In our team medical bag, I had a large bottle of aloe vera. It certainly wouldn't cure him but might soften some of the scar tissue. I asked her if she would come to the church that evening for a worship service, where I could give it to her. The interpreter shared the sad news that the woman did not think her husband would permit her and her son to come.

That evening, I looked for them, but did not see her or the child. At the end of the service, the little boy came up to me and tugged on my sleeve. He and his mother had come. I introduced them to the pastor, and a physician who directed the organization that sponsored our team. The doctor thought he might be able to arrange help for the child when a surgical mission team would come later in the year.

Today, that boy is thirteen, walking normally and attending school. He hangs around whenever we have a mission team there, and his parents and entire family have joined the church.

* * *

## Learn and Serve

Whether the mission of your team involves construction, teaching, evangelism, medical care or some other type of project, your primary goal is to *learn* and *serve*. Choose team members who have the willingness and flexibility to learn and to serve others. Such openness allows them to approach others in friendship, offering a hand-up rather than a handout.

An amazing transformation occurs within your team as well as those you are serving when you approach them as equals, as friends, as brothers and sisters in Christ. Going into another's world as friends gives them an opportunity to receive us without loss of their own self-esteem. Be a team who encourages, uplifts, reaches out to others in the name of Jesus Christ to share God's love and grace.

## 10 Commandments for Learn and Serve Team Members

1.  Honor God in all you do, say and wear.

2.  Pray and ask others to pray for the team and the people you will serve.

3.  Be thorough, correct and prompt with all paperwork and payments.

4.  Remember always that you represent your team, your church, your country and God.

5.  Refrain from wandering, or going out alone. Valuable time can be lost searching for you, not to mention what might happen to someone who separates from the team.

6.  Be low key. Do not draw attention to yourself or your group by loud behavior, actions or clothing.

7.  Be humble. You are there to learn and serve, not to fix anyone, or teach a "better way of living."

8.  Leave your own major life issues at home.

9.  Learn the rules and obey them. Your country's laws

are not necessarily the same, and if you break the law, even unintentionally, you can jeopardize yourself, the entire team, your hosts, and future mission endeavors.

10.  Offer to help the Team Leader.

* * *

*Since there will never cease to be some in need on the earth, I therefore command you, "Open your hand to the poor and needy neighbor in you land."*
Deuteronomy 15:11

## Action Plan

### Personal response:
We don't ask others to change; **we** change so that they can hear the Word of God.

### Awareness:
How will you invite team members so that their answers are "Yes!"

### Making a Difference:
Choose your target, task and begin to build a team.

# Chapter 5

## Team Building

*You first receive the dream by faith. Then it becomes reality.*
*Each day must count for the dream.*
*Be faithful in the small things that work toward the dream.*
Esperance, a missionary from Rwanda

### Vision

No matter what the project is, <u>people</u> come first. A short-term mission begins with the leader's vision of how to make a difference in people's lives, while accomplishing a task.

When a group of people comes together, however, they don't function as a team just because someone has recruited them, or shared the idea of a mission project with them. To bring them together, the team needs to acknowledge a common purpose. The leader may assume that everyone has the same goal, the accomplishment of the project, but that isn't automatically the case.

Initially, each team member will have a different personal goal, perhaps learning about Third World countries, or "helping others," or "sharing God's love." Moving from varied individual goals to the team's common objective requires listening to and acknowledging members' various objectives before presenting the vision for the team. Invite your team to discuss their goals and show them how the team's goals encompass each person's individual objectives.

If you were to write a mission statement for your team, it might sound like this:

*"To serve people in a way that is practical and relevant to their needs, that initiates life changes, and creates a desire to follow Jesus Christ."*

This sums up the objectives of any short-term mission, whether the project involves construction, conducting Bible School, providing medical care or performing street evangelism. Serving others, meeting their needs is the core of short-term missions. When the focus is on people, not place or task, lives are changed.

Within this mission statement, there are several important concepts. First, a short-term mission is all about serving people, following the example of Jesus Christ.

*For even the Son of Man did not come to be served, but to serve, and to give his life as a ransom for many.*
Mark 10:45

A short-term mission shares God's love in practical ways because telling people about God's love is never as effective as showing them His love. Actions speak louder than words.

Meeting "their needs" does not mean what <u>we</u> perceive they need, but keeping in mind always that a short-term mission project belongs to the people we are serving. They own their problems and they need to own the solutions. When you cross cultural boundaries, you may encounter lifestyles that are very different from your own. It can be very difficult to see another lifestyle and not judge it in terms of right and wrong. Try, instead, to refrain from using those words and accept that the lifestyle or culture is merely different than yours.

55

Of course, that is not to say that there are never wrong aspects of any culture. Physical, emotional and sexual abuse of women, children, the elderly or vulnerable are never right or acceptable.

What is different is what we consider abuse. In our culture, very young children are not left home alone all day while parents work. In many other countries, leaving children on their own can be more common and even necessary. If you see something which troubles you, ask your host what the social customs or normal practices are.

## Hunger, Homelessness and Poverty

Poverty also brings a whole set of challenges, fears and prejudices. How do you answer questions about poverty?

- What is our responsibility as Christians to help those in need?
- How can we share the Word of God if we do not first share the Love of God?
- Why are people poor?
- Why don't they have a house? (or shoes, or jobs, or education)
- Why does a man stand on the corner with a sign asking for money?

How can you examine poverty without politicizing it, without finger-pointing, without feeling helpless, angry or guilty? Americans often take pride in being people who "pull ourselves up by our bootstraps." We expect each generation to be better off than the preceding one. We expect most people to reach their full potentials and lead creative, productive lives. We accept these conditions as the norm and don't really comprehend people who do not or cannot live like we do.

The Bible tells us plainly that God will not hear our prayers if we close our ears to the cries of the poor. We should expect, therefore, that the church in America will not experience blessing and revival unless we care for the poor and needy. Meeting physical needs opens the door for sharing Christ. For believers, that's what God expects of us.

The difference between a short-term mission project and just doing something nice for someone is the intention to change lives. When God's love is shared, especially without any expectation of returns, lives are changed.

"Creating a desire to follow Jesus Christ" is always the goal. However, the mission may be a seed-planting one in which the team doesn't see the harvest. God, then, is responsible for nurturing what you have sown.

## Relationships vs. Task

In our Western culture, we want to see numbers—how much of the building did we complete, how many shingles did we lay, how many bags of cement did we use, how many children came to VBS, how many people prayed and accepted Christ, how many toothbrushes did we give away. We are task-oriented and time-focused. We would much rather reap the harvest than plant the seeds.

But, short-term missions begin and end with relationships—the relationships your team members form with each other, how they work together to serve people at the project site, and the friendships they form with the people they meet. Building relationships is the long-term impact of the short-term mission. With this mindset, you can view the project with God's eyes. As you develop objectives for your team, set aside the numbers and outcomes and focus on people.

On a recent medical mission trip, I was reminded of relationship vs. task. On these missions, I want to know how many people we treat each day, how many doses of antibiotics we use, how many pairs of glasses are fitted. I bring home all of the patient forms and enter the information in a database so that I can know the ages, diagnoses, treatments and referrals of our patients. I justify this curiosity with the value of statistics for planning the next trip.

Two weeks after the trip, I pulled out the forms to put them into order for entering into the computer. The first twenty-five forms from the last morning of the clinic were missing, probably left in the office where they had been taken for copying.

And God reminded me again, it's not the numbers that counts in His world. It's the 14-year-old child who was being abused and now that her secret has been exposed, can live without the shame and fear, and get the help she needs. It's the 8-year-old girl blind from birth who is started on the path of diagnosis, surgery and possible cure. It's the little boy whose emergency surgery will enable him to have children someday. It's the mother who faced medical problems in her pregnancy and got immediate help.

I overheard Dr. Bill in the clinic asking his patients about their education, their jobs, their household living conditions. He took time with each person to learn about them, their hopes for the future, their dreams. He encouraged the youths to continue with their schooling, the teens not to rush into motherhood, the elderly not to worry about normal aches and pains.

It's about the smiles, handshakes and hugs of arrivals and departures. It's about the puppets and bubbles shared with children while they wait to see the doctor, and the gummy bears that chase away the nasty taste of parasite pills. It's about the songs, memory verses and craft projects that will stick in children's memories for years. It's about enjoying the meals someone else has prepared for us, and the worship service shared with us.

It's about understanding that, although we come from a different place and culture, we have so many of the same problems and concerns, family issues, and worries. But we also share the same love of God, and on a mission trip, get to express that one person at a time.

**The primary goal of every short-term mission is transformation: the building relationships, first by getting**

**to know each other, then learning to reach out to others, and finally, growing closer to God as His child.**

## Diving Board Dilemma

Your team goals describe both a future state and a call to adventure. Enthusiasm and excitement can sweep along team members through months of meetings and preparation, but at some point, each individual faces a moment of personal commitment. This need for commitment places the team member on the end of a mental diving board, weighing the pros and cons of jumping.

Every team member (and perhaps even you, the leader) can experience one or more diving board moments. Obstacles can begin to cloud the vision, causing doubts to arise, and motivation to wane. The person wavers, unable to jump or to back away.

Team leaders must have the vision for themselves, but they must also have the ability to encourage others to adopt the vision and goals as well. Continuing to present the goals to the team, explaining structure, direction and the roles each member will play, will address fears and questions that immobilize team members.

Encouraging members to feel attachment to the group as something greater than the sum of all its members holds out hands to catch the person at the end of the mental diving board. When you, the leader, establish an atmosphere in which all team members feel a shared responsibility toward the team, group harmony and interpersonal growth proceed. Give the team opportunities to contribute, to learn from and work with each other, to share ideas, experiences, feelings, and fears with each other.

## Sample Team Goals

Medical Team:
> We will set up a temporary clinic to provide medical, dental, vision and pharmacy care for people who need care, regardless of their religion, culture or ability to pay.

Construction Team:
> We will partner with a community for their building project.

Teaching Team:
> We will help local teachers conduct Bible School for the children of the community.

For all Teams:
> We will open ourselves to a learning experience in another culture by serving God and His people. We will love God, love others and serve both.

## Team Building

You hear it with every team: "Why do I have to come to meetings?" Often, the inexperienced team members complain the most (and skip meetings more frequently). In the first few years, we tried to vary the meetings, offer something new each year. That didn't seem to help.

Now, we use the same pattern and content for meetings every year. What works for us now is the returning team members (usually about 50% of the team) who generate so much enthusiasm about being together again, both here and on the mission field, that all catch their spirit, and new members want it also.

Unity as a team is inclusive, but not exclusive.  Every year, we have team members who have been on one or more previous short-term mission teams.   There is a natural inclination to reminisce, to share stories and private jokes.  We try to limit that so that new members feel welcome and included, and are able to enjoy the experience without prejudice.   Instead of indulging in past experiences use the memories to illustrate some point, such as the dangers of wandering away from the group.

We all know how easy it is for cliques to form, and how damaging they can be to a church.   Be sure to include everyone in every activity.  Unity in the midst of the diversity of individuals with different talents, strengths, weaknesses, ideas, experiences, beliefs, personalities, backgrounds, goals and agendas is crucial for the team.  The team cannot share God's love with a needy world if they do not have love for each other.  The leader sets the tone for how the team relates to each other and to the people to be served.

Encourage each member of the team to begin a personal journal.  Participating in a short-term mission is a journey of faith.  Documenting experiences, prayers, feelings, or just using the pages to record the lists of supplies to pack can be valuable.  For many team members, this will be the first time they have kept a journal.  Remind them not to get hung up on spelling or grammar – a journal is between you and God.

A journal does not have to be a diary, or even a day-by-day rendering of what has transpired on the trip.  I am always grateful when I come home with a detailed accounting, but many days, I am too busy and too exhausted to write much.  My husband uses a small notebook to jot down important things, usually in one word or a short phrase throughout the day. He is the one who keeps track of names and email addresses, places and what we ate. I tend to write my thoughts and impressions and get side-tracked with wordy descriptions.  Together, we have a wonderful (and complete) account of the trip (when I am not too tired to write).

A separate journal for the team is also very valuable. Our teams used the same journal for four years. During the periods of preparation and the weeks of the short-term missions, the book was passed from person to person for their thoughts, recording of events, diary of the day, prayers and memories. The journal documented the work and the personal growth of the teams. We shared it with new members from year to year, we laughed over favorite memories, we mourned the loss of one of our team members who died several months after her third STM.

We consider the team journal so important that we assign one person the job of "Journal Keeper" with the responsibility of passing the book and including every team member. Even those who have not kept their own personal journal will usually participate in the team journal. I am always the one who writes the first entry and my husband concludes the entries a few weeks after our return.

## Ideas for Building Team Unity

1. Have a meal together, a potluck, an International dinner, or eat at an ethnic restaurant.

2. Participate in a local mission project to prepare for your STM, for example, a Christmas party for local Hispanic migrant farmers. or serve meals at a local soup kitchen.

3. Hold a fund-raising event to benefit the team, the project or a separate mission organization.

4. Celebrate the team, enjoy a social event, picnic, party, or do something fun as a group.

5. Include time for devotions, study and prayer in your meetings, rotate responsibility for meditations among all team members, plan devotionals while on the STM.

6.  Start a team journal or a scrapbook, create "baseball" cards with a team photo and share them with others as prayer-reminder cards.

7.  Create team luggage tags or luggage ties.

8.  Hold a cross-cultural event, invite a career missionary to one of your meetings, schedule a training workshop.

9.  Have a Send-off or Welcome Back ceremony with the organization or church sending the team. If you are flying to the STM, travel together to the airport.

10.  Give each team member index cards with the name of another team member on each card.  Ask team members to write a prayer, or a word of encouragement for that team member, then give the team the cards while on the project.

* * *

*Above all, love each other deeply, because love covers over a multitude of sins.*
1 Peter 4:8

# Action Plan

### Personal response:
Define team goals.
Move the team from individual personal objectives to team goals.
Start your own personal journal and team journal.

### Awareness:
Build trust with information about logistics, roles and responsibilities, task details.

### Making a Difference:
Involve others in raising spiritual & financial support, & collecting supplies.

# Who Am I that I Should Go?

# Chapter 6

## Finances and Fund-Raising

*Involve God first in all you do.*

### Team Budget

Early in the preparation process, the team leader will need to establish a budget for the team and project. Communicating with the in-country hosts will help you to determine the daily living costs and any extraneous expenses.

| Team Expenses | Project Expenses |
|---|---|
| Round-Trip Airfare | In-country Transportation |
| Transportation to and from Airports | Daily Living Expenses (food, accommodations) |
| Pre-departure Expenses (printing, postage, phone, meetings, fund-raising) | VBS Materials |
| | Project Supplies, and Tools |
| | Gifts for In-country Hosts |
| | Interpreter's Fee |
| Visas, Departure Tax, Airport fees | Tips for Hotel Staff, Airport Porters, Bus Drivers |
| | Sightseeing |

| Baggage fees | Team First Aid Kit |
|---|---|
| Travel Insurance | |
| Miscellaneous | |

## Financial Questions

One of the first questions team members will ask is: "How much will the trip cost?"

To determine the cost per person, add all of the expenses and divide by the number of team members. Team members may also incur personal expenses for passports, immunizations, physician appointments for medical clearance, clothing and luggage, airport meals and snacks, airline baggage fees, and possibly their own in-country tourism or shopping.

How will team members pay for their expenses? Will each person be responsible to secure all of his/her own finances? Will the group hold fund-raisers to benefit the entire team or divide the proceeds equally among the participants? Will "scholarships" provide help for persons with greater needs? How will team expenses such as project materials, VBS supplies, postage and printing be paid?

Our teams use a combination of funding methods. Some team members pay their entire expenses; some receive assistance from their churches or from family and friends. The team often holds fund-raising events to assist those who need help or to obtain funds to purchase project supplies.

The primary reason to hold a fund-raiser, however, can be the opportunity to begin developing team unity.

# Food & Fun

Combining food, fun and fund-raising has been often highly successful for us. While the team works together on the project, they can raise money and awareness of the mission. Traditional dinners, such as Spaghetti, Ziti or Barbecued Chicken, work well because you can prepare large quantities of food with simple recipes and ingredients. Try to get the supplies donated and hold the dinner at a free site, such as a church. Youth often enjoy serving, or providing child care for an adult "date-night" dinner. A holiday such as Valentine's Day is a perfect occasion to schedule a special meal.

\* \* \*

## A Luncheon Idea

A church friend, hearing of Barbara's involvement on a STM, asked if she could prepare a luncheon as a fund-raiser. They scheduled the meal in the church Fellowship Hall, following the late-morning church service. Several weeks before the luncheon, Barbara invited the STM team leader to speak and pre-sold more than 80 tickets for $10 each. Several others who were unable to attend the luncheon donated the money anyways.

After a meal of chicken salad, rolls, brownies and beverages, the team leader presented a slide show, video and talk about the mission project. She mentioned during her speech that one of the goals of this team was to give each child a 6-month supply of vitamins, but that would cost about $500. At the end of the presentation, the pastor rose and suggested that if each person in the room gave $6, there would be enough money for the vitamins.

People began tossing money on a table, and when the pastor counted it, he had $824. All together, Barbara raised more than $1000 for her own trip expenses and nearly as much for medical supplies for the team.

\* \* \*

Consider charging a family rate to encourage more people to attend a meal, or providing take-out service. At one event more take-out than dine-in barbecued dinners were sold.

## Ideas for Meals

- Offer a meal of beans and rice, with tortillas or pita bread. A majority of the world's population lives on rice, or beans, and simple breads. Use the opportunity to educate about world hunger and poverty issues.

- Hold an international dinner with foods from other countries or from the country your team will visit.

- Prepare 2 meals: a simple meal with rice and a cooked vegetable, and a typical American dinner. Serve every tenth person the American meal; everyone else receives rice and vegetables. Discuss how much more we eat in variety and quantity than people in Third World countries.

- Have weekly Soup Suppers with a different type of soup and bread each time.

- Try a "Picnic-on-the-grounds" if you have the space at a church or a nearby park. You provide grills and ask people to bring potluck dishes to share or a meal for their own family. Raise money by selling drinks, or auctioning desserts.

- Auction brown bag lunches.

- Sell Super Bowl Subs on Super Bowl Sunday.

- Hold an ice cream social with home-made or purchased ice cream and a selection of toppings.

## Selling

When we were raising funds for a youth group trip to England, we sold nearly anything anyone could think of. Pecans, even during the Christmas pecan-pie season, were not a big hit. Candy at Valentine's Day did only slightly better. Perhaps there is some niche product your community craves. However, you have competition from schools who sell wrapping paper, books and magazine subscriptions, and Girl Scouts with the corner on cookies.

## Ideas for Sales

- Sell "shares"-- typed documents which enable the bearer to "share" in the mission endeavor.

- Sell coupons donated by local merchants and restaurants.

- Hold a Rummage Sale, Garage Sale, or Book Fair.

- Have an in-home product demonstration party and arrange to donate a percentage of the sales to the team.

## Service

"Rent-a-Kid" was one of our better fund-raisers. Every Saturday, the youth offered their services doing chores for a donation. They painted, cleaned, pulled weeds, baby-sat, pressure-washed driveways, and mowed lawns. Most of the time, they were paid more than they'd have earned had they set a fee for their work.

## Ideas for Service

- Wrap gifts during the holidays.

- A large department store hired youth as Holiday Greeters top open doors, greet shoppers, and carry packages to cars.

- Instead of, or in addition to a traditional car wash, hold a "pet wash."

- Clean car windows in the church parking lot during a service. Sell tickets in advance and ask the purchaser to place the ticket under a wiper so that you don't wash the windows of people who either don't want it or have car alarms turned on.

## Special Events

If you have access to musicians, bands, or entertainers, a show is a great way to raise money and generate publicity. Schedule a concert at a fund-raising dinner, picnic or ice cream social. Talent shows, your own version of a singing or dancing competition, can be fun and profitable. Be sure to sell refreshments as well as charging admission.

## Ideas for Special Events

- Hold a "Sock Hop" for adults or teens. Price of admission is the donation of a pair of new socks for the mission field. Sells refreshments, or provide babysitting to raise funds.

- Show a movie. Do not charge admission since that violates the law. But you can sell refreshments and charge for childcare.

- Provide a Family Game Night with games for all ages, some inexpensive prizes, and of course, refreshments for sale.

- Have a carnival with games, food, face-painting, etc.

71

## Social Media

Facebook® provides a perfect place to conduct fund-raising events. You have access to your family and friends and friends of your friends. You can create any sort of virtual event to ask for donations, or auction items, or invite people to attend a fund-raising event. Holly collected about twenty donated items and held an auction for several days on Facebook®. People bid against each other and at the deadline, the top bidder received the item. They paid online and Holly shipped the items to the winners. She made several hundred dollars for her mission trip.

A blog enables you to keep in touch with your team, friends. family, church, or team sponsors as you prepare for the trip, serve on the project site and return.

## Sponsors

In every church, there are members who are willing to meet a need, whether large or small, but often anonymously. Ask people to "adopt" or provide a "scholarship" for team members. Use a tree branch, or a Christmas tree with cards or ornaments listing specific needs. People can take a card from the tree and meet that request. For example, "$25 for in-country transportation," or "$15 for one day's VBS supplies." Be specific in the requests, and include items with a wide range of cost.

## Ideas for Sponsors

- Create "baseball cards" for each team member or the team as a whole to use as prayer reminders, and for requests for financial support.

- Adopt-a-missionary; sponsor a team member with $5 or $10/month for a year. Pay into a church-designated fund as credit toward expenses for a future mission trip.

72

- Plan a dinner after the trip to thank the donors and share the trip with them. They'll be more likely to support the next trip if they can see and experience the results of their donation.

- Create a print, email or online newsletter or blog to involve your sponsors in your planning, trip and return home.

## Donations

Church members, family and friends often want to participate in Short-Term Missions, but cannot personally go on the mission. Give them opportunities to support the team with prayers, finances, or materials. One team sold printed certificates of "shares of stocks" to support their team. Shareholders were invited to a special dinner after the team returned from their project.

Think beyond money when asking for donations. For example, people who live on a fixed income might be able to contribute hand-made knit baby clothing, craft supplies for VBS, used eyeglasses, or empty, cleaned medicine bottles. Make a list of the needed supplies and put a box for donations in the church lobby (doctor's or dentist's offices, workplace, etc).

Encourage team members to send a letter to family and friends requesting both prayer and financial support. Many of our team members use this approach to obtain funds for their trip expenses. Small donations of $5-$25 add up quickly and allow your family, friends and church members to participate in your project as supporters.

\* \* \*

## Sample Support Letter

*Dear*
*I'd like to share with you an exciting adventure I am going on in October. I will be working with a medical mission team to provide care for about 500 people in Ecuador. For most of these people, this will be their only opportunity for medical care this year.*

*Our trip is being coordinated by _____ (organization name). Our team will share God's love in practical ways as we address poverty and malnutrition, along with preventable diseases.*

*I hope you will consider becoming one of my ministry partners. Please pray for me as I prepare for this mission, and especially during the week of October 19-26, 2011 as I travel and work in Ecuador.*

*We are raising money for the expenses of the trip and the necessary medical supplies. The trip costs approximately $____ per person. We also take medications and school supplies with us. If you are able to support this project, please send your **tax-deductible** contribution to _____.*

*Will you join me as a partner in ministry? Thank you for your support and helping me as a prayer and/or financial partner in this mission.*

**＊ ＊ ＊**

# Surprise!

There are always unexpected expenses for teams and team members. Try to anticipate these when you begin recruiting team members. Passports, immunizations, tips for servers or drivers, airport parking fees, transportation to the airport, airport departure taxes in foreign countries can easily add several hundred dollars for the individual or team budget. Team members need to know whether they will need any shopping or spending money if occasions to spend will arise.

Consider also where and when you will exchange money. It may be possible and advisable to exchange money before you leave the U.S. Check with your bank or travel agent or in-country host for advice. Some airports have kiosks where you can change money. Often a kiosk in an airport in the U.S. is less expensive that changing once you arrive in country.

Your host can answer questions about using traveler's checks. Where we usually go, traveler's checks are not widely accepted so we don't bother with them.

You will also need to know whether you can use credit cards in the host country. The rules for each bank can vary so be sure to check with your credit card company about any hidden fees for using a card out of the country.

## A Personal Note on Finances

As I write, we are going through a recession with one financial crisis after another, and more and more bad news about economic recovery. Over the last few years, we have seen team members work harder and harder to raise funds. Churches have less money coming in, and are less likely to support missions. Many people question our priorities, pointing out that there are needy people here at home. There is no denying that the world is hurting. But, no matter how difficult it is for us, it is far more desperate for those in Developing Countries. In the U.S., we have safety nets most of the world does not know. We have Social Security, Medicare, Medicaid, unemployment insurance, retirement accounts, social and charitable organizations providing assistance in almost every community. When I am tempted to complain about the huge increases in airfare, or gas or food costs, I must stop and remind myself how much better my life is than in most of the world.

God is the cure for the worry and fear about finances. He wants my availability, not ability. This is the lesson when it comes to raising funds for individual or team expenses. God is in control of my life and my finances. When I surrender my life, my finances and my availability to Him to use me as He sees fit, He will supply my needs. You can trust Him to supply yours as well.

\* \* \*

*But seek first his kingdom and his righteousness,*
*and all these things will be given to you as well.*
*Therefore do not worry about tomorrow, for*
*tomorrow will worry about itself.*
*Each day has enough trouble of its own.*
Matthew: 6: 33-34

## Action Plan

### Personal response:
Seek God's guidance through prayer about fund-raising needs and plans.

### Awareness:
Establish a budget for the team and project; determine the cost per person.

### Making a Difference:
Decide how the team will raise funds; begin fund-raising.

# Chapter 7

## Development

*Give a man a fish, feed him for a day.*
*Teach a man to fish, feed him for a lifetime.*
Chinese Proverb

For those who have much, it is so easy to give. We feel good; we think the people who receive our gifts should feel grateful. God wants us to share His love in practical ways. Everyone wins.

God wants us to share His love in ways that affirm people, inviting them to grow, and giving them hope for the future. Whenever possible, helping others help themselves should be our goal. There is a place for relief—the provision of needed materials and assistance during and immediately after an emergency or natural disaster. However, most of what we do on Short-Term Missions should be aimed at development, rather than relief. Short-Term Mission teams who act like Santa Claus are less likely to help the people they are serving, and they can set up an expectation that future Short-Term teams will bring bigger and better gifts.

How can you reconcile the desire to improve lives with a way of giving that preserves their self-esteem and allows them to be partners, rather than children, in the relationship?

| Relief | vs. | Development |
|---|---|---|
| • Meets immediate needs in emergency<br>• Provides services<br>• Initiates short-term change<br>• Gives temporary relief<br>• Focuses on Individuals<br>• Involves donor-recipient relationship<br>• Offers a generic plan<br>• Fosters dependency<br>• Helps others<br>• Provides a handout | | • Assists people to meet their own needs<br>• Provides tools to develop services<br>• Changes lives long-term<br>• Aims for self-sufficiency & sustainability<br>• Fosters community partnerships<br>• Establishes fraternal relationships<br>• Acknowledges local perceived needs<br>• Encourages empowerment<br>• Helps others help themselves<br>• Provides a hand up |

* * *

On the first day on the construction site, two team members decided to replace a wobbly wheelbarrow used to transport concrete from the cement mixing area to the place where the sidewalk would soon be. They asked one of the local workmen how much a new wheelbarrow would cost and persuaded him to take them to buy one. Without checking with the leaders of their team or the project supervisor, they headed off to a store and bought a new wheelbarrow

The old wheelbarrow had been adequate, although not a Cadillac. In their rush to do the work with greater efficiency, the men substituted their solution for what had been working within the context of the local environment.

* * *

Another team had collected $150 to be used for "some need in-country." The team leader mentioned it to their host and asked her to suggest how best to use the money. She suggested they buy beads for a group of women making necklaces to start a micro-enterprise selling them.

While the team had many other ideas for the money, they followed her suggestion. She took them to a small store in someone's home where they selected the beads and a few tools for this beginning business.

On the way back to the project site, the host asked the team members to help think of a name for the women's co-operative and their fledgling business. They came up with "Sister-to-Sister," or "Hermana a Hermana" in Spanish. A few days later, she brought the team some necklaces the women had made. Their price was $5 each, but the team knew the necklaces were worth more. They bought all of them and marketed them for $10 each. Within a month, they had collected $1200 to send back to the women.

With that "seed" money, the women's group re-stocked supplies and created more necklaces. Soon, they were able to purchase three treadle sewing machines, expand their business to include hand-sewn purses. As their confidence and self-esteem grew, they set up parenting classes and Bible studies, and began to send their children to school.

Later, as empowered women, they took on injustice and political corruption in their community. Eventually, they were instrumental in bringing electricity to their neighborhood. With new skills and work, they've helped other women leave lives of prostitution. With assistance from other mission teams, a daycare center and church were built around the efforts of this women's co-operative. To date, the Hermana a Hermana Project has impacted the lives and families of more than thirty women, their children, families and their community.

## Teaching a Person to Fish

Development often involves education. Is there an opportunity to teach a skill at the project site (no matter what type of project you are doing)? Often, you only need offer and an opportunity can be set up. Consider what simple lessons you might offer.

## Health Teaching Topics

- Dental hygiene, brushing and flossing, with locally available supplies
- Basic First Aid
- Cleaning and bandaging a simple laceration
- Applying pressure to a bleeding wound
- Splinting a fractured bone
- Caring for a burn
- Nutrition during pregnancy and lactation
- Handling choking emergencies, the Heimlich maneuver
- Cardiopulmonary resuscitation
- When to seek medical help
- Treating rashes and other skin problems
- Checking temperature and pulse
- Treating frostbite, or heat exhaustion
- Treating dehydration, nausea, vomiting or diarrhea
- Mixing Oral Re-hydration Formula using locally available products
- Treating insect and snake bites
- Bringing down a fever
- Identifying and treating for lice
- General nutrition

- Combining protein foods
- Sprouting seeds and using sprouts in the diet
- Preventing spread of infectious diseases, especially sexually transmitted diseases
- How to use eye drops
- Treating childhood illnesses, such as mumps, measles, chicken pox, the flu
- Preventing or managing diaper rash
- Caring for a baby, child or elderly person
- Preventing sexually-transmitted diseases

## General Teaching Topics

- How to swim, drown-proofing a child
- Basic sanitation, how to disinfect water
- Hand-washing
- Child development
- Nutrition, fitness

## Appropriate Technology Teaching Topics

- Creating and managing a compost pile
- Raised bed, wick, container or rooftop gardening
- Making an adobe brick press
- Water pumps
- Water purification systems
- Building a simple stove
- Solar cooking/water heating

## Teaching How-To's

One year, we created videos to show children how to brush their teeth. My daughter made a video of her children using a hose outdoors for a water supply to brush their teeth. They loved the opportunity to brush their teeth in the backyard. Trying to hold a hose and toothbrush and toothpaste all at the same time was challenging and the toothpaste ended up in the grass.

They, then, moved to the bathroom for a more detailed explanation of proper tooth-brushing technique. Everything was proceeding well until the youngest one, then 3, decided she wasn't getting enough video coverage. The tape actually turned out very well and was quite humorous.

We arranged to have a DVD player and television at the mission project site. But getting the children to watch the video proved to be a problem. They were unaccustomed to watching television and preferred the coloring books in the waiting area.

Teaching in another culture, let alone in another language, can be a challenge. Printed materials won't work if your audience cannot read. Discussing family planning is illegal or culturally unacceptable in some countries. Teaching about certain topics might not be possible when children are present.

Careful advance planning and preparation are essential. Begin with researching the needs with the host organization. They can also provide help in determining the best teaching method to employ.

You might organize lessons or you may engage in simple, directed conversations. Often, the best approach is to present material person-to-person as a friend. We are not experts in how another culture should live. Even though I am a nurse, I try to present lessons as a mother or woman sharing with others.

Sit with the group arranged in a circle if possible, so that you are on the same level. Encourage free-flowing discussion and questions so there is an open exchange of information. You are a learner as well as a teacher when you are in another culture.

## Teaching Methods

- Photos
- Video, DVD (if equipment is available)
- Posters, Pamphlets
- Models
- Demonstrations
- Child care, Tooth-brushing, Heimlich
- maneuver,
- CPR
- Puppets
- Drama
- Music

## Enabling Others

Information, getting to know someone, leads to compassion. Compassion demands action. Jesus Christ saw people in need and took practical action to meet their needs.

Development means giving your presence and the presence of God, rather than presents. Development improves conditions of knowledge, skills, and attitudes helping people to improve their environment and lives.

Development recognizes the worth of other people, encouraging them to solve their own problems and meet their own needs, perhaps with assistance, but always preserving their self-respect. When you approach others as a friend, development is part of the relationship. Hope is the outcome. Development means moving from *doing for others* to *doing with others* with the goal of enabling them to *do for themselves.*

\* \* \*

*If you have any encouragement from being united with Christ, if any comfort from his love, if any fellowship with the Spirit, if any tenderness and compassion, then make my joy complete by being like-minded, having the same love, being one in spirit and purpose. Do nothing out of selfish ambition or vain conceit but, in humility, consider others better than yourselves.*

*Each of you should look not only to your own interests, but also to the interests of others.*
Philippians 2: 1-4

# Action Plan

### Personal response:
How will your team promote development?

### Awareness:
Consider how you can partner with the host community to meet the needs they have identified.

### Making a Difference:
Develop lessons, or a Bible study, either in the language of the host culture, or to be used with a translator.

# Who Am I that I Should Go?

# Chapter 8

## Santa Claus

*I no longer call you servants, because a servant does not know his master's business. Instead, I have called you friends, for everything that I learned from my Father I have made known to you.*
John 15:15

George brought a bag of cookies on a Short-Term Mission trip and passed them out one morning at the project site. He made sure everyone there—the team, the work crew and the children--got one. About an hour later, one of the children returned and handed the team leader a quarter.

"For the cookie," he said.

The leader gave it back to him. "No, you don't have to pay for the cookie."

A few minutes later, the child's mother arrived and insisted the leader take the quarter. "It's okay," he tried to tell her. "We were all eating cookies and it wouldn't have been polite for us to not offer him one. This is far too much money to pay for one cookie."

She smiled and nodded but refused to take back the money. Finally, an interpreter explained, "She wants to pay for the cookie because she needs to show her child how not to become a beggar."

The leader accepted the quarter then and thought about how a small chocolate chip cookie had almost undone their week's work and team testimony without their even knowing it.

## How to Give

There are safe and sensitive ways to give. *Always give to the leadership of the host organization.* Allow them to determine where and how to share your gifts. Do **not** give to individuals. It's hard not to respond to appeals, but fraught with problems if you do. Set a rule and share it with your team. You will not give items or money to individuals, including, for example:

- clothing you plan to leave behind when you go home
- coloring books to the children in VBS
- cookies or candy or chewing gum
- an admired item, tool or work gloves that you really don't need
- money for desperately-needed medical care
- promises you will do something after you return home.

There are appropriate ways to give. When a team brought shoes to give to the local pastor, he set up a work program in which youth might "earn" a new pair by doing small jobs around the church. If team members want to leave some clothing at the end of the trip, check with your local host to see if that is acceptable and always give a few dollars to pay for cleaning. Giving dirty, used clothing is not acceptable in any society.

Instead of giving toys during VBS, do a craft project. When children create a craft and take it home, they will remember the lesson longer. Instead of passing out candy and cookies, which are not healthy snacks to begin with, use the money for school supplies.  A school or community center can use all the books, crayons and toys you can offer.  Give to the teachers and let them decide when and how to share things with their students.

If you have funds to give, ask how your hosts would like to use the money.  They know best what they need, and you should abide by their decision.  One team thought a pre-school nursery should have rocking chairs and offered to buy one.  The director of the program preferred to purchase mirrors for each classroom.  She explained that a single chair might only accommodate one adult and one or two babies for a few minutes, while a mirror would allow each child in a class to learn grooming skills.

We are often, by nature, problem-solvers.  We have much to give and we want to share.  When a situation arises, first explore all of the options available within the community with its indigenous resources.  Communicate with the hosts.  If something, such as tools, need to be purchased locally, follow their advice and lead.  Does the situation require a wheelbarrow, or is another method actually better in the long run?

## Cookies, Candy, and Snacks

We are a people who enjoy snacking and sweets.  We are also generous and share these with others.  But eating between meals might not be acceptable or advisable in other cultures. Check with the host organization before bringing food with you. If you need to eat between meals because of a medical condition, perhaps you can find a private moment alone.  If not, be sure to share your food with everyone. When you do offer food, ask parental permission, if possible, before giving any to children.

## When Giving Makes Sense

The Short-Term Mission team has opportunities to give items appropriately. A medical team provides medications, diaper cream, perhaps medical supplies, such as toothbrushes, within the context of caring for patients. A team visiting an orphanage might bring baby clothes, diapers and toys. Again, keep in mind, you are giving to the host or organization, not individuals.

On one trip, we decided to give aprons to the kitchen staff who cooked for us daily. Good idea, but we took the wrong number and someone's feelings were hurt. Now, we bring small kitchen implements or towels as a gift for our hosts, rather than individual items for each person preparing and serving the meals.

If you are taking gifts for your hosts, consider choosing items which are unique to or representative of your community. We have taken baseball caps with our church's name on them, a box of candy from a local chocolate company, postcards with pictures of our city, and a photo book with pictures from previous teams. When we watched the growth and change of a community as a daycare center was built over several years, we collected the pictures from those years and made a memory book for our host. These are the types of gifts you would take to a friend.

## When to Be Cautious

Patrice, a nineteen-year-old university student served as a translator for a team. She made friends quickly and began email correspondence with a team member. When she asked if he could send her a pair of jeans, he sought advice from the team leader.

On the surface, it seemed to be a reasonable request and not prohibitively expensive. However, the situation was fraught with potential problems. Giving gifts to one individual in a community can cause jealousy, hard feelings and friction in the community.   Expectations of gifts can also undermine the work of the next Short-Term Mission Team.   In this situation, there was the additional complication of the age and gender difference between the correspondents.  Even in our culture, a friendship between a fifty-year-old divorced man and a female college student might be viewed as inappropriate.

The team member explained that he could not send her the pants.  The young woman continues to correspond with several members of the team.

* * *

On her first mission trip, Ellen carried a small bottle of alcohol gel with her everywhere, as she had been instructed.  When she had used all of the gel, rather than throw the bottle away or return it to her suitcase, she gave it to a child at the project site.

The team leader reminded her that she had been asked not to give anything to anyone but the project host.  Even though the empty plastic bottle was trash in Ellen's eyes, it was a commodity in Haiti.  Ellen had caused a problem in giving it to one child. Every child and woman at the site now expected to get one.

* * *

There are people whose needs are desperate and tragic, and there are times when you want to and can help. Before you act, think about the best way to help, talk over your plans with your host, missionary or pastor.  During nearly every trip we meet a child who needs advanced treatment, whether surgical, dental, vision or therapy. We might have the financial means with us to provide that care, or the ability to go home and raise the funds. Decisions about when and how to give funds are always difficult. We have provided money through the pastor or our host, a physician, when we were able and the pastor or physician agreed it was the right decision. As I write this, we are in the process of trying to arrange surgery for a blind child we met on our last trip. The decision to help her is made even more difficult by the fact that there are no guarantees surgery will help her. It is very hard not to approach the situation from "if this were my child, I would do everything and anything to restore her sight." Ultimately, she is my child.

\* \* \*

## Santa Comes to Town

Total strangers from another country drop in to visit you for a week.  You aren't sure if your accommodations meet their expectations, or if your food is good enough for their palates.  Throughout the week, they ply your children with candy and goodies.  You don't want to risk offending them even though your children have tummy aches and refuse to eat the meals you have prepared.

When your visitors leave, they give you many gifts.  Clothing, not new, but clean and not too worn.  You would like to have had the jacket they gave your neighbor.  After all, he already has a coat and you have none.  The t-shirts they gave your family have words on the fronts, written in their language, and you hope the sayings are not offensive.  The shoes are too large for anyone to wear.  But you keep them and wear them anyway.

What have you learned from their visit?

They are rich.  God has blessed them well beyond anything you will ever enjoy.  They are generous.  You could never give as they have given.  You hope you do not owe them now. They probably didn't like your food since they ate so much of what they brought with them.  The clothing is nice, even if it doesn't fit, and is not what you would ever choose to wear.  They never asked what you might need.

Only the shoes are a problem. After a few attempts to wear them, you put them on a shelf in your home so that everyone will know you have friends from another country.

# Who Am I that I Should Go?

\* \* \*

*And they did not do as we expected, but they gave themselves first to the Lord and then to us in keeping with God's will....But just as you excel in everything—in faith, in speech, in knowledge, in complete earnestness and in your love for us—see that you also excel in this grace of giving.*
II Corinthians 8: 5, 7

## Action Plan

### Personal response:
How will your team handle giving?
What can you give children other than sweets?

### Awareness:
How can you help someone to *become* more rather than
to *have* more?

### Making a Difference
Changing lives, like charity, begins at home.

# Chapter 9

## Paperwork and Passports

If you are working with a sending organization, you may have paperwork to complete for them. If not, create your own forms to capture information you will need.

```
                 Suggested Forms

    1.  Registration form
    2.  Release from Liability in the event of an
        accident
    3.  Medical Information and Release
    4.  Physician's Examination form
    5.  Background check
    6.  Copy of the Passport photo page
    7.  Adverse Event form
```

Instruct team members to **always** use their names *as they appear on their Passports* to on all of your forms. When the airline issues a ticket, the name on the ticket must match the name on the Passport.

Always make several copies of completed forms: one for your sending organization, one for your records and additional copies, if needed, for travel insurance or other purposes.

## Registration Form

Record the information needed to contact your team members: name (as it appears on the Passport), nickname, street address, home, work, cellular and fax numbers, email address, Passport number and expiration date. Possible additional information includes birth date, nationality, next of kin or emergency contacts, occupation, employer, and the name of the member's church. Including birth dates allows you to send a card if the birthday comes before the trip.

You can create a separate spread sheet with contact information for the whole team for quick access to addresses and phone numbers, and then, share it with team members so that they can keep in touch with each other.

## Release from Liability Form/
## Adverse Event Form

While no one ever wants an adverse event to occur on a Short-Term Mission trip, accidents happen. Information on this form is needed in the event of emergency hospitalization or death. If the sending organization doesn't have a Release Form, create your own to protect yourself. If you have any youth on the team, you will need a Parental Consent and Release Form for those members. Even if a parent accompanies the team, you should still include a Release Form, in the event the parent is not with the youth at all times.

## Medical Information and Release Form

Team members should disclose any medical conditions or disabilities that may impact them or their work, including environmental, food and medication allergies. Include the name, phone number and policy number of the member's health insurance company, who is the responsible party for medical expenses, and physician contact information. Team members need to check their insurance coverage regarding

out-of-network, or out-of-country coverage. Medical insurance can be purchased from some travel insurance companies.
Each team member should authorize a person on the team to act as a medical surrogate, to give consent for medical treatment or surgery in the event the member is unable to consent. You may want to have this form notarized.

Of course, you hope you will not need to ever use these forms, however you must be prepared for any unforeseen situation. On my last mission trip, I ended up going to an emergency room with a possible kidney stone. Our in-country host was a physician who accompanied me. Because we had my paperwork with all of my medical history and information, a great deal of time was saved and confusion avoided.

## Physician's Examination Form

We require team members to have a doctor evaluate their general health, make recommendations for immunizations, or medications, and provide a signed release prior to an overseas Short-Term Mission. The physician may not be familiar with the specific conditions of the location, so we offer information based on the recommendations of the Volunteers in Mission Medical Fellowship. Most doctors will follow these suggestions for immunizations and prophylactic medications. The U.S. Department of State website also has recommendations for the health concerns for specific countries.

## Background Check Form

A sending organization may require a background screening of all team members. A local police or sheriff's department can advise you how to proceed, or you can use a company such as Lexis Nexis, P.O. Box 812289, Boca Raton, FL 33481. You may also consider asking for a letter of reference or recommendation from members' pastors.

## Passport Photo Page

Obtain a copy of the Passport photo page from each team member. In the event a Passport is lost or stolen, this copy will become invaluable in procuring a new Passport. Be sure to pack these papers and carry them with you at all times. Team members should also make a copy for themselves, and carry it along with two extra Passport photos. To obtain a new Passport, you must have photos identical to the ones on the original.

On a trip to China, one of the team leaders lost her passport the night before the team was to leave the country. She had an extra set of photos and a copy of her passport, however, she needed a replacement of her visa to leave. Even expedited, issuing a replacement took a week. Another leader stayed with her and the team proceeded to leave without them. Make contingency plans for the added costs should this happen to one of your team members.

## Other Forms

Team members who bring their own prescription medications should carry a copy of the prescriptions with them (separate from the pill bottles). Those who wear glasses may also want to bring a copy of the lens prescription.

## Wallets

Carry as little as possible and you risk loss of as little as possible. Instruct team members to clean out their wallets before they go. Leave behind unnecessary credit cards, voter registrations, library cards, club I.D.'s, frequent diner cards, etc. If you have your Passport, you won't need your driver's license (unless you will be driving to or from the airport). If you plan to drive in another country, you can obtain an International Driver's License from the American Automobile Association

(AAA). Check with your automobile insurance company about your coverage.

## Passports

Your Passport documents your citizenship and provides some protection, primarily the right to re-enter the United States. You will need a Passport book to go abroad, with the exception of travel by car or boat to Canada, Bermuda, Mexico and the Caribbean. For those countries and means of travel, you may use a Passport Card instead of a Passport book.

Application for a U.S. Passport is not difficult, but can be time-consuming; you should allow two-to-four months for a new application and one-to-two months for a renewal. The demand for Passports is seasonal with peak times between January and July. If you need the Passport within three weeks, you can expedite the processing for an additional fee. If your needs are even more urgent than three weeks, you can make an appointment at a regional Passport Agency. You will need proof of your travel date.

**You are never charged a fee for an appointment at a Passport Office.**

The Application for Passport (Form DS-11) may be obtained online or at one of more than nine thousand facilities such as post offices, libraries, U.S. embassies, courthouses, municipal facilities and Passport Agencies. Complete the form as instructed but, **do not sign the form** until you file it with a Passport Acceptance Agent.

## Documentation needed for a Passport Application

- Proof of Citizenship (1 of these)
  Previous Passport
  Certified Birth Certificate, with
  registrar's embossed seal, signature and date

100

(persons born in Washington D.C.
will have a Birth Certificate card)
Naturalization Certificate, or
Certificate of Citizenship

- Proof of Identity (1 of these)
    Previous Passport
    Naturalization Certificate
    Current Driver's License
    Current Government or Military I.D.

- Passport Photos (2)
    2 inches x 2 inches, identical, taken
    within the past 6 months
    Color, with white background
    Full face, measuring 1 inch to 1 3/8 Inches
    from the bottom of the chin to the
    top of the head
    Wear normal attire, no uniforms, no
    hats or headgear, no sunglasses; you
    may wear a wig, glasses, hearing aids

- Passport Fee(2012) (credit cards and checks accepted)
    $110 first time applicant + $25
    execution fee
    $ 80 minors + $25 execution fee
    $110 renewal
    $ 60 additional fee if expedited

# Youth

Minors under the age of sixteen must appear in person to apply for a Passport, along with both parents or a legal guardian present. If only one parent is available, a notarized Statement of Consent (Form DS-3053) to obtain a Passport is required from the absent parent. If the parents are divorced, the parent accompanying the minor to apply for a Passport must have documentation of sole custody.

Youth must also have a picture I.D. (see Proof of Identity above) and proof of relationship (such as Birth Certificate) listing both parents' names. Parents must present their own identification and co-sign the application for youth without a picture I.D.

## Passport Photos

You can obtain Passport photos at camera stores, drugstores or take your own at home with a digital camera. If you take your own photos, follow all of the requirements for size, background and attire. When you have your Passport photos taken, purchase at least one extra set. Carry these along with the photocopy of the picture page of your Passport. If you lose your Passport, you must have photos identical to the one on the original for a replacement.

You might need additional Passport photos for Visa application, or for travel cards within the country.

## Application Process

Fill out the forms, but **do not sign the application** until you appear at the Passport Agency or Acceptance Facility. Take your identification, Proof of Citizenship, photos and fees to a Passport Agency. You will also need your Social Security card; the IRS may impose a $500 penalty if you do not provide your SS number.

Renewals and change-of-name can be handled by mail.

When I changed my name after marrying, the Passport Agency typed the new name on the last page of the Passport book. Of course, no one bothered to look for the name change, and I always had to explain why the name on the photo page and the airline ticket were different. Finally, I tucked a copy of my marriage license into my Passport.

## Guard Your Passport

A United States Passport is worth a great deal of money on the black market in many countries, therefore, guard it carefully when you travel. A Passport carrier or wallet, especially one that can be secured inside your clothing, is an excellent way to carry it. Keep a copy and the extra photos in a separate, safe location in your luggage or purse.

You will need your Passport at the airport when you check in, when you go through security, and at Immigration Control desks. Some hotels request to see your Passport when you check in, and banks or Money Exchange facilities may also require it.

## Visas

Many countries require a Visa, a document which indicates that you have met conditions to enter the country for a specific purpose, such as tourism, education, business, temporary employment, transit to a third country, etc. You must obtain a Visa from the Embassy or Consulate of the country you intend to visit. Each country has different requirements for application, such as proof that you have a residence, job and bank account in the U.S. (indicating you will return home), proof of wellness, a host address in the country you will visit, proof you can support yourself, health and evacuation insurance. Check with the Embassy or Consulate for requirements, fees and applications.

Some countries are sensitive about the purpose of the visit. You may want to state "tourism." "Missionary" is often expected to be a full-time vocation with a longer visit time and perhaps some special work permit. In some countries, especially where Christians are in the minority, it can even be dangerous to classify yourself as anything but a tourist. Check with your hosts about what is best.

Americans traveling to a country in which the U.S. does not have a Consulate or Embassy, can often obtain help with Visa applications through the Swiss Embassy.

## Registering with the U.S. Embassy

The U.S. Government offers travel registration as a free service to U.S. citizens who are traveling to, or living in, a foreign country. You will receive advance information about civil unrest, terrorism warnings, health concerns or natural disasters. Registration also enables the U.S. Embassy to assist you in the event of an accident or illness while you are traveling, or if your family needs to contact you in an emergency. Registration is voluntary and free, and your information is confidential.

---

For Information about Travel Restrictions and
Embassy Registration
www.travel.state.gov

---

## Action Plan

**Personal response:**
Decide what information you will need for your team
and begin collecting it.

**Awareness:**
Register with the embassy of the country you will visit.
Apply for your Passport (and Visa) if needed.

# Chapter 10

## Planes, Trains and Automobiles: Traveling Safely

> *"We aren't in Kansas anymore."*
> Dorothy to Toto,
> *Wizard of Oz*

### Before You Go

Traveling safely begins before you leave home. Just as you plan what to pack, also plan what to leave behind, including valuables, especially jewelry and watches, irreplaceable family heirlooms, unnecessary credit or debit cards and any forms of identification you won't need on the trip.

### Other Items to Leave at Home

- A copy of your itinerary, including emergency contact numbers

- A copy of your Passport photo page, your airline tickets and both sides of any identification cards and credit cards you are carrying

- A copy of the serial numbers of travelers' checks

- Expensive camera equipment and electronic equipment, such as music devices, cellular phones (unless it is a satellite phone or has international calling).

## Traveling Light

Mission teams often go to places where there are no elevators to rooms on the fourth floor, where streets aren't paved, where ground transportation is a van or small car. These trips remind me of commercials for indestructible suitcases because bags get tossed, dropped in puddles, dragged across cobblestones, sat on, and stacked on the roofs of buses. Duct tape has saved several suitcases in mid-trip.

Packing light means traveling easily, quickly and with one hand free. Airlines charge for overweight bags and many are also now assessing additional fees for all of your checked bags. Check with your airline for the size and weight restrictions. We weigh each bag at our packing party to avoid surprises at the airport.

In addition to the outside identification tag, put your name, address and telephone number inside each suitcase, backpack, camera bag and purse. Use a brightly-colored fabric tie—in a color other than red which is the most common color for suitcase markers—to mark all of the bags belonging to team members. One year, the neon-orange tie saved us from losing our bag of tools when we spotted it under a pile of luggage being wheeled out of baggage claim by a thief. Now, when our flight arrives, some members of the team pull bags off the luggage carousal while others guard the pile of suitcases until all have been collected.

Never leave bags unattended in public places, including the hotel lobby. Use the buddy system to watch your bags, or take them with you to the restroom, shops or snack bar.

## Safety on the Street

If you have a spare wallet dedicated to travel, you don't need to clean out your everyday one. You might use two billfolds for travel. One holds a little money and the other has your identification cards and most of your money. If robbed, you can surrender the one with a few dollars in it and hope the thief gets away without realizing there might be more.

Purses, tote bags, fanny packs and the outside pockets of backpacks or clothing are easy targets for pickpockets and thieves. Keep money, valuables and your Passport close to you in the inside pocket of a backpack or jacket, in a sturdy purse with the strap across your chest, or in a pouch or money belt worn under clothing.

There is security in numbers. Encourage team members to stay with a buddy at all times, including restroom visits in airports and restaurants. In many cultures, young women do not travel without a family member or chaperone. If you have young women on your team, assign a partner who will give the appearance of being a chaperone.

Be cautious in areas where you might be victimized: markets, festivals, tourist sites, crowded subways, elevators, narrow alleys and transportation stations. Try to avoid travel at night whenever possible.

Scam artists, pickpockets and thieves make their living from tourists. Even children can be pickpockets or create a diversion that assists a thief. Be wary of anyone who approaches you, speaks English, offers directions or to be a guide, or tries to sell you something. Frequently, pickpockets work in teams with one person distracting you by jostling, asking a question, creating a disturbance, or spilling something on your clothing. Alert team members who watch out for each other, can stop a purse-snatcher or pickpocket.

One of our team members had her camera stolen from her pocket by a child pickpocket on a sidewalk even though she was with a group of team members and knew to be cautious. Zip your pockets, put your camera strap around your wrist and your hand in your pocket, or carry it in a safer spot.

In a car, bus or van, keep your hands inside, and the window les than half-opened. A watch can be quickly snatched from your wrist or a purse or backpack from the seat through an open window. Whenever the bus or car parks, put belongings you plan to leave, under the seats or in the trunk. Be hyper-vigilant at all times.

* * *

## An Experience

The bus driver parked immediately in front of the church located in a high crime district. We only had twelve feet of sidewalk to cross from the bus to the church entrance. Both doors opened simultaneously, and we scurried into the safety of the building. When it came time to leave, team members were less cautious. They formed a line and took their time, backpacks and purses dangling from shoulders as they walked toward the bus. Suddenly, a man came running at the line of women. At the same time, another man approached from the opposite direction. A team member at the rear of the group stepped up, raised his hand, and, in a loud voice, commanded, "Stop!" Both strangers halted in their tracks, then turned and fled.

* * *

## Street Safety Tips

- Assign 2 people to be "Trailers" and bring up the rear of the group to keep an eye out for potential trouble.

- Try to avoid walking along the curb, but if you must, carry your purse on the opposite side and always with the strap across your chest.

109

- If you are taking photographs, ask someone to keep an eye on you and your belongings while you are pre-occupied.

- Don't tell strangers where you are staying.

- If you are confronted, give up your decoy wallet.

- Use a sturdy backpack or purse. Leather is harder to cut through than fabric.

- Avoid public demonstrations and civil disturbances. The police and soldiers will not take the time to identify non-participants.

## Attracting Attention

Your goal is to avoid becoming a target by not looking or acting like an affluent tourist. Affluence is not usually a problem for mission teams, however, you also may not want to look like a mission team. Keeping a low profile in appearance and behavior can keep the team from drawing the wrong type of attention.

We don't have team shirts for several reasons. We want to be inclusive both at home and at a mission project site. In dressing alike, the team sets itself apart from others, and that is not the message we want to give. We also think it is safer when traveling to avoid wearing shirts or caps with slogans or identification markings. If you wear a name tag at the site, be sure to remove it when traveling to and from the site.

## Hotel Safety

Keep the door locked at all times and do not open it without checking the identity of the person outside. Don't assume it is another team member.

Do not leave valuables out in the open in your room. While you cannot lock your suitcase at the airport, you can lock it in your hotel room. In some cultures, an item left on a bedside table or bathroom counter signals that you are done with it and you don't want it any more. If you cared for it, you'd put it away. So, by leaving it out, you are inviting someone to take it. Before you leave, check the room for an alarm clock left on the table, shoes by the bed, vitamins and make-up in the bathroom.

### In Case of Emergency

- Know the exits, the stairs and the way out in case of fire.

- 9-1-1 doesn't work outside the U.S. Ask the desk clerk how to summon help.

- Establish a place outside the hotel where team members can meet in an emergency.

- Know what conditions are likely for the place you are visiting: earthquakes, volcanic eruptions, tsunamis, politic unrest and how to respond.

## Traveling Wisely

Use that decoy wallet when buying things in public so that you don't appear to be carrying large wads of cash. Be as cautious about your credit card as you are at home.

If you use a taxi, check the price before you get in, especially if it does not have a meter. Frequently, the hotel desk clerk can summon a taxi for you, but he may receive a kickback from the driver so be cautious and only use one with a meter.

Americans have been arrested for buying souvenirs which have turned out to be antiques, determined by authorities to be national treasures. Be careful when shopping and know both the local laws and the U.S. Customs regulations.

When you are in a foreign country, you are subject to its laws. You can be arrested for actions that may not be illegal in the U.S.

If you drive in another country, you may want to have an International Driver's License (available through the American Automobile Association). Familiarize yourself with traffic laws and customs, especially right-of-way which may be different than what you are accustomed to.

Renting a car can be very challenging. Before you leave home, check with your credit card company. Most recommend you decline additional collision insurance, however, this is not an option in some countries. You could have an unpleasant surprise when you arrive and find out you must pay several hundred dollars cash for insurance on the rental car.

Be cautious with your camera also. You can also be detained for photographing anything or anyone the government does not want photographed, including airports, military installations and personnel, government buildings, police, border crossing points, political demonstrations, and embassies. Churches and museums may also request that you not photograph their artwork and displays.

## Traveling Politely

Try to remain low-key in airports, restaurants and on public transportation. Encourage the team members to save joking around, loud conversations and group prayer for private places.

Recently, our local news reported for several days about the trial of a woman accused of attacking another woman whom she thought had cut into the line at a children's ride at Disney World. Each report mentioned that the attacker was visiting the park with a church group.

It is a sobering thought that, on a Short-Term Mission, your behavior can reflect not only on you, but also on your mission team, your church, and your country.

Leaving your comfort zone means more than leaving a favorite recliner in front of the television. The experience on a Short-Term Mission can be physically, emotionally and spiritually exhausting. Traveling, whether at the beginning or end of the trip, adds its own set of demands.

One of our teams experienced this at an airport when a team member got into an argument with an airline representative. What began as a simple miscommunication because of language differences, quickly escalated to the possibility the entire team could have missed the flight home.

We try to prepare our teams for the possibility of delays, diverted landings, missed connections, long flights, and unscheduled stops due to engine problems. What we can't anticipate is how people will behave under trying circumstances.

* * *

*Your attitude should be the same as that*
*of Christ Jesus.*
Philippians 2: 5

# Action Plan

### Personal response:
Assign Trailers for team travel, and chaperones for all young women.

### Awareness:
Learn where your team will be staying and how the team will travel in-country.

### Making a Difference:
Discuss expectations of behavior in different situations. Develop a plan for emergency situations.

# Who Am I that I Should Go?

# Chapter 11

## Team Health Concerns I: Before You Go

### "What Shots Do I need?"

This is the first question and sometimes one of the greatest fears of Short-Term Mission team members. Whether in the U.S. or abroad, you will need certain immunizations, many of which you have probably already received. Most vaccines require a few weeks to build immunity within your system, so start them at least four to six weeks prior to your departure.

One exception, Hepatitis B vaccine, requires a six-month-long series of three injections. If you don't have six months before your trip, go ahead and begin the series as soon as you can.

### The 3 R's

The Centers for Disease Control and Prevention (CDC) divides immunizations into three categories: **routine, recommended and required**. You have probably already received most of the routine vaccinations, but you might need boosters to increase your immunity. Check with your physician. The vaccinations listed below represent those **routine** immunizations Short-Term Missioners should have.

| Routine for Adults ages 19-50 | Routine for Adults over 50 yrs |
|---|---|
| Tetanus-Diphtheria-Pertussis (Td or Tdap) | Tetanus-Diphtheria-Pertussis (Td or Tdap) |
| Hepatitis A (2 injections over 6-18 months) | Hepatitis A (2 injections over 6-18 months) |
| Hepatitis B (3 injections over 6 months) | Hepatitis B (3 injections over 6 months) |
| Varicella (If you haven't had chickenpox) | Varicella (If you haven't had chickenpox) |
| Measles, Mumps, Rubella (MMR) | Shingles (if you have had chickenpox) |

## Category 1: Routine Immunizations

On a Short-Term Mission involving a construction or building renovation project, you need a **Tetanus** booster if your last one was more than ten years ago. Tetanus (Lock-jaw) is caused by bacteria entering through any break in the skin. Most cases occur in people over fifty years of age because boosters have not been kept up-to-date.

The Tetanus vaccination often comes with immunizations for Diptheria and Pertussis (Whooping Cough). You can obtain the injection from your physician or the local Health Department. The best time for this shot is four-six weeks prior to travel.

## Hepatitis Alphabet Soup

Hepatitis is a serious liver infection caused by several different viruses (designated A, B, C, D, and E), transmitted through different routes. The infection usually causes flu-like symptoms, jaundice, severe abdominal pain and diarrhea. Long-term chronic liver disease and liver failure may result from any Hepatitis infection, necessitating a liver transplant.

All types of Hepatitis can be found throughout the U.S. and the world. Check with your physician of the CDC website (information at the end of this chapter) to determine if you need a vaccination for Hepatitis A and/or B. There are no vaccinations for the C, D or E.

| | | |
|---|---|---|
| **Hepatitis A** | Spread by close personal contact, or through contaminated water or food, especially shellfish | 2 injections, at least 6 months apart May experience injection site soreness, headache, loss of appetite, tiredness lasting from 1-3 days |
| **Hepatitis B** | From unprotected sex, exposure to infected blood, or needles, or transmission from a mother to her baby during birth | 3 injections, over 6 months May experience injection site soreness, headache, loss of appetite, tiredness lasting from 1-3 days |

| | | |
|---|---|---|
| **Hepatitis C, D** | Acquired through unprotected sex or exposure to infected blood or needles | No vaccine |
| **Hepatitis E** | Spread by contamination food and water; found primarily in Southeast Asia and North Africa | No vaccine |

## Category 2: Recommended Immunizations

Whether you need any of the recommended vaccinations depends on your destination, the season of the year, your age, general health and previous immunizations. Check the CDC website for specific instructions.

| Possible Recommended Immunizations |
|---|
| • Typhoid<br>• Rabies<br>• Polio |

## Typhoid

Although Typhoid can be contracted in any country, South Asia, Africa, the Caribbean, Central and South America present the greatest risk of exposure to travelers. You get the infection from food or beverages handled by a person who carries the bacteria, or from sewage-contamination of water used for drinking or washing food. CDC guidelines recommend vaccination for visitors going to smaller cities, villages, and rural areas off the usual tourist paths.

Symptoms of Typhoid infection usually develop within one week and include persistent, high fever up to 104° F (40° C), headache, fatigue, loss of appetite, stomach pain, enlarged spleen, rash of flat, rose-colored spots, and slow heartbeat. The illness can be treated with antibiotics and you will feel better in two-three days.  Persons who have had Typhoid, although recovered from the acute illness, continue to carry the bacteria and can infect others.

Typhoid vaccination involves one injection, repeated either in 2 years or in 5 years, depending on the type of medication give. Schedule the injection at least one week prior to departure.

## Rabies

Rabies is transmitted through the saliva of *any* mammal, with dogs and bats being the most common carriers of the disease. The period between infection and the first symptoms is normally two to twelve weeks, but can be as long as two years. Death almost always occurs within two to ten days after the first flu-like symptoms.

Symptoms progress to difficulty swallowing, hypersensitivity to light and sound, fear of water, weakness progressing to paralysis, delirium, convulsions followed rapidly by coma and death.

All animal bites or scratches must receive immediate treatment, beginning with a thorough cleansing of the wound using copious amounts of soap and water.  Treatment requires five injections of Rabies vaccine over a twenty-one day period.  Do not interrupt the series even if you experience side effects.

Persons who expect to be exposed to Rabies can receive one injection of the vaccine in advance.  If exposure occurs, the series will be completed at that time. Rule-of-thumb: do not touch stray dogs or cats or any other animals in other countries.

# Polio

Poliomyelitis is an acute viral disease of the Central Nervous System, transmitted by contact with an infected person. It has been eradicated in most countries of the world. If you are traveling to Africa, Southeast Asia, or the Middle East, check with the CDC to determine if you need a Polio booster.

If you were born in the United States, you most likely have already received vaccination which confers lifelong immunity. Travelers to areas where polio cases are still occurring should receive the vaccine, if they are unvaccinated.

## Category 3: Required Immunizations

The CDC lists only **two** required immunizations, both related to *where* you are traveling. Saudi Arabia requires vaccination against **Meningococcal** disease for travel during Hajj.

## Yellow Fever

If you visit certain subtropical countries in Africa and South America, you must have immunization against **Yellow Fever**, a viral disease transmitted to humans through the bite of infected mosquitoes. Symptoms vary in severity from a flu-like fever to jaundice, severe liver infection, organ failure, or hemorrhagic fever progressing to death. The disease occurs in sub-Saharan Africa and tropical South America. Because deaths have occurred among unvaccinated tourists, all travelers are required to show proof of immunization when visiting countries where Yellow Fever occurs.

Schedule the vaccination at least ten days before travel. If possible, get together with several others for the vaccination because the medicine often comes in a multi-dose vial and the vaccination clinic will appreciate havign several injections at the same time. Immunity lasts for ten years. The immunization will be recorded on an International Certificate of Vaccination (yellow card) that should be carried with your passport

Do not take the injection if you are allergic to egg-based vaccines; your doctor can give you a Letter of Waiver to carry with you. Contact your local Health Department to locate an immunization clinic.

# Malaria

One other disease requires advanced preparation to prevent infection: malaria. Female *Anopheles* mosquitoes carry a parasite which, when introduced by a bite, infects red blood cells, causing symptoms of light-headedness, shortness of breath, rapid heart rate, fever, chills, weakness, nausea and general muscle aches. In severe cases, coma and death can occur.

No vaccine is available; however, oral prescription medications prevent infection in most cases. Your physician can recommend which one of several medications is best for you, and give you a prescription. Follow the prescription directions, beginning the medication one week prior to departure. Complete the entire schedule of doses, which can take up to four-to-six weeks, depending on the medication your doctor prescribes. If you discontinue the medication early, you can become infected.

Preventing mosquito bites is the primary way to prevent Malaria infection.

- Stay indoors at dawn and dusk when mosquitoes are most active.
- Wear long-sleeved shirts, long pants and clothing that minimizes exposed skin.
- Apply insect repellents containing Permethrin to clothing, shoes, tents, mosquito nets, and other gear for greater protection. Permethrin cannot be used directly on skin.

- Use a repellent with DEET on skin. Apply sunscreen first, then insect repellent.
- Always sleep with a Permethrin-treated mosquito net tucked in around the bed.

Mosquitoes carry other infectious diseases, including:

- Dengue Fever
- Japanese Encephalitis
- West Nile Encephalitis
- Chandipura
- St. Louis Encephalitis
- Equine Encephalitis
- La Crosse Encephalitis
- Murray Valley Encephalitis
- California Encephalitis
- Russian Spring-Summer Encephalitis

Sometimes misdiagnosed as influenza, the symptoms of Dengue Fever include sudden onset of fever, severe headache, muscle and joint pains, stomachache, nausea, vomiting and diarrhea. Occasionally, a bright red rash appears on the lower limbs and chest. The illness lasts up to seven days. There is no vaccination to prevent Dengue Fever, and the infection can be spread from person to person through blood exposure.

Persons with Encephalitis experience fever, headache and sensitivity to light, as well as weakness, seizures, and neck stiffness.

No vaccines are available to protect against these illnesses, therefore, avoiding mosquito bites is the best way to prevent infection.

## HIV/AIDS

If ever there was a situation that requires the hope of salvation found in Jesus Christ, it is the HIV/AIDs worldwide pandemic. No matter where you are going on your Short-Term Mission, you are likely to encounter someone whose life has been affected by this disease.

Acquired immunodeficiency syndrome (AIDs) describes a set of symptoms and infections resulting from the damage to the immune system caused by the Human Immunodeficiency Virus (HIV). The disease leaves persons more susceptible to infections and tumors. Transmission of HIV occurs during unprotected sex, exposure to blood or body fluids, and from mother to child during birth or breastfeeding.

> For More Information about Diseases and Immunizations:
> Centers for Disease Control and Prevention (CDC)
> 1600 Clifton Rd, Atlanta, GA 30333
> (404) 498-1515 or (800) 311-3435
> www.CDC.com

## Action Plan

### Personal response:
Contact your physician or Health Department and begin immunizations.

### Awareness:
Check with the CDC about health concerns specific to the country you will visit.

### Making a Difference:
Make a personal plan to control your exposure to mosquito-borne disease, if you will travel to climates where mosquitoes are present.

# Chapter 12

## Team Health Concerns II: Staying Healthy

Whether you call it "La Turista," "Montezuma's revenge," or "Traveler's Diarrhea," you have plenty of company in your misery. The CDC reports up to 50% of international travelers contract this "most common illness." It can strike during the first week of travel or after you have returned home. Bacteria, usually E coli, contaminate food or water causing the infection characterized by abdominal cramps, nausea, vomiting, diarrhea, bloating and malaise which lasts for several days. While the illness itself is usually not life-threatening, you can become dehydrated quickly, feel miserable, and miss out on the mission activities.

Prevention is the best way to avoid infection. Remember these rules:
- "Boil it, cook it, peel it or forget it."
- The Rule of "P's:" Food is safe if it is
  Peelable,
  Packaged,
  Purified, or
  Piping hot.

Thoroughly wash unpeeled fruits or vegetables with soap and bottled, treated, or boiled (and cooled) water. Peeling a fruit or vegetable means removing the skin without touching the part you will eat, for example, peeling a banana. When you peel other fruits, such as an apple, the first time a knife blade cuts the peel, the blade picks up the bacteria. On the second pass, the knife spreads the germs all over the fruit you are about to eat.

## Preventing Traveler's Diarrhea

- Avoid tap water, ice, salads, raw vegetables and fruits that cannot be peeled.
- Avoid mayonnaise, unpasteurized dairy products, shellfish, raw or undercooked meat and seafood.
- Tie a ribbon around the bathroom faucet to remind you not to use the water to brush your teeth.
- Use bottled, treated, or boiled (then cooled) water to brush your teeth.
- Hum in the shower so that you don't accidentally get water into your mouth.
- Wash your hands with alcohol hand gel or packaged wipes, especially *after* you wash them with tap water, and always before you eat.
- Do not eat food purchased from a street vendor or in an establishment that doesn't appear clean and sanitary.
- When in doubt, pass it up.
- If it isn't cooked, think twice: the lime juice in ceviche (fish soup), for example, does not kill bacteria in the raw seafood, and an alcoholic drink does not kill the bacteria in ice.

## Treating Traveler's Diarrhea

Traveler's diarrhea will often resolve without specific treatment, but, oral re-hydration with clear liquids, or sports drinks can replace lost fluids and electrolytes. If nausea, vomiting, abdominal cramps, fever, or blood in the stools continue beyond 48 hours, you may need an antibiotic. The CDC suggests 500 mg of Ciprofloxacin twice daily or 400 mg of

Norfloxacin twice daily for 3-5 days.

Speak to your own doctor about the advisability of taking preventive antibiotics. The CDC does not recommend taking antibiotics unless you become ill, but some physicians, including the Volunteers in Mission Medical Fellowship, suggest using Ciprofloxacin once a day to prevent diarrhea while traveling.

Over-the-counter Bismuth Subsalicylate (Pepto-Bismol®) is the most effective treatment for persons who are not allergic to aspirin, pregnant or taking certain other medications. Check with your physician or pharmacist before you go, about any possible medication interactions in case you need to use Bismuth Subsalicylate.

## How to Take Bismuth Subsalicylate

- To prevent diarrhea, take 2 tablets of 262 mg. 4 times daily or 1 fluid ounce 4 times daily.
- To treat diarrhea, take 1 fluid ounce or 2 tablets of 262 mg every 30 minutes for up to eight doses in a 24-hour period.
- This regimen can be repeated on second day.
- Watch for these common side effects: dark tongue, tarry stools and ringing in the ears.

## What about Anti-diarrheal Drugs?

Some physicians believe diarrhea is the body's defense mechanism to get rid of harmful bacteria quickly. Anti-diarrheal drugs, called anti-motility agents (Loperamide, Diphenoxylate, and Paregoric) treat diarrhea by slowing the action of the bowels. If you have fever or bloody diarrhea, do not use these medications because they can increase the severity of the disease by delaying clearance of pathogenic bacteria.

Finally, tell the team nurse, first-aid person or team leader if you develop diarrhea because someone needs to know to watch for symptoms of dehydration or other complications.

---

Homemade Oral Re-hydration Solution

1 teaspoon of salt
8 teaspoons of sugar
1 quart of clean or boiled water (then cooled) water
 if available, add ¼ teaspoon of salt substitute (potassium)

Stir the mixture till the salt and sugar dissolve.

---

## Filtered, Boiled, or Disinfected

E coli isn't the only culprit in water. Other bacteria, protozoa, viruses, spores and parasites also cause water-borne illnesses. In the absence of single-serving bottled water, any water you drink or use for washing must be filtered, and boiled or disinfected.

**Filtration** involves pouring water through a barrier of paper, cloth, ceramic, charcoal, or sand to remove gross particles, dirt and parasitic eggs. Viruses and bacteria remain, so the water must still be boiled, or treated with chemicals before drinking or using it.

**Boiling** water is the method of choice for treatment. Reaching and maintaining a temperature of 60°C (140°F) for five to ten minutes kills disease-producing organisms. The water must then be stored in a container that has been previously disinfected with boiling water or chemicals to avoid re-contamination.

A low-cost alternative to boiling water over a fire is solar heating. Water placed in a clear bottle or plastic bag in direct sunlight purifies within six hours.

**Disinfection** requires treating filtered water with chemicals such as Chlorine, or Iodine. You can purchase water-treatment products at camping supply or sporting goods stores.

---

Take Home Message

- Water must be cleaned by filtering before boiling or chemical disinfection.
- Always purify the container to be used for storing the disinfected water.

---

## High Altitude Illnesses

The oxygen level in the air decreases the higher you climb above sea level. If you're planning a Short-Term Mission at altitudes over 8,000 feet, you may experience symptoms of High Altitude Illness (also called mountain sickness). Symptoms of High Altitude Illnesses begin within one to two days at high altitude. Persons who have heart disease or chronic pulmonary disease may notice symptoms at altitudes lower than 8,000 feet, and may have more serious effects. Staying at a high altitude for a few days allows the body to acclimate to the lower oxygen level, and eases symptoms of hypoxia (decreased blood oxygen).

High Altitude Illnesses

- Acute Mountain Sickness (AMS)

- High-Altitude Pulmonary Edema (HAPE), which affects the lungs

- High-Altitude Cerebral Edema (HACE), which affects the brain

| Symptoms of AMS | Symptoms of HAPE | Symptoms of HACE |
|---|---|---|
| Headache Breathlessness Fatigue Nausea and Vomiting Insomnia Swelling in the face, hands, legs, or feet | Extreme fatigue Severe breathlessness at rest Fast, shallow breathing Cough, possibly with frothy or pink sputum Gurgling or rattling chest sounds | Confusion Behavioral changes Lethargy Loss of coordination or balance Staggering |

## Take Your Time

Gradually ascending is the best way to avoid or lessen the effects of high altitude. That is not be possible when flying into a high altitude airport such as La Paz or Quito. In that case, take it easy for the first forty-eight hours to allow yourself to become accustomed to the altitude.

At a high altitude, eat a high carbohydrate diet, drink extra fluids, (about 1-1/2 gallons per day), avoid tobacco, alcohol and medications such as sleeping pills that depress the respiratory system, and can worsen symptoms.

Using your favorite headache medication and a decongestant nasal spray will also help minimize the initial effects of high altitude. Your physician can also prescribe the medication, acetazolamide (brand name Diamox®).

Common side effects of this drug include numbness and tingling in the fingers and toes, more frequent urination, and the need to drink more fluids to avoid dehydration and headaches. A person who is diabetic or allergic to Sulfa, should not use this medication.

HAPE and HACE can be *life-threatening*. If someone begins to experience the symptoms of HAPE or HACE, immediately move the person to a lower altitude for twenty-four hours. The person may try to ascend again more slowly, but if symptoms return, he should remain at lower altitude.

\* \* \*

## General Health Tips

- On long plane flights, bus or train rides, exercise your legs at least once every hour to prevent deep vein thrombosis (DVT)-- blood clots in the legs.

- Presume every child has a respiratory infection and try to avoid letting them get too close to your face. Your own family members are reservoirs of respiratory germs, but because you live with them, you have some degree of immunity. Other countries have a whole new set of germs.

- If you have allergies requiring an EpiPen®, be sure at least one other person on the team knows where it is and when and how to use it.

- Wash your hands with alcohol gel frequently.

- Stay out of the water. Swimming and wading may be hazardous to your health because of parasites, leeches, water snakes, carnivorous fish, etc. in the water.

- Do not touch animals. Besides the risk of rabies, parasites, ticks, and fleas found on animals all carry diseases.

- Apply insect repellent to your ankles and feet and wear socks at night to prevent bites from bed bugs.

- A diabetic going to a high altitude location, needs to check with the glucometer manufacturer. Blood glucose levels can register differently at high altitude.

## Packing Personal Meds

When you pack personal medications, they must remain in their individual labeled prescription or over-the-counter bottles. Carrying a copy of your prescriptions is also advisable. If you use any narcotics, or opioid medications or anything unfamiliar, ask your physician for a letter verifying the prescription and instructions. Pack any medications you must have daily in your carry-on bag.

## Way Out of Network

Your health insurance may cover you on a Short-Term Mission, but it may not offer the same coverage you normally have. Check with your insurer before you travel to avoid unpleasant surprises. Medicare and Medicaid do not provide coverage outside the U.S. and its territories, or Mexico and Canada. You can get a Medi-gap insurance for traveling.

Consider purchasing a travel insurance policy to cover out-of-pocket medical expenses. As a bonus, you will also get trip-cancellation, delay, lost baggage and other protections.

For more Information on Travel Insurance
- Contact TravelSafe Insurance, P.O. Box 7050, 40 Commerce Dr., Wyomissing, PA 19610, (888) 885-7233, www.travelsafe.com
- Compare policies at www.Insuremytrip.com

Other Medical Concerns and Travel
- International Association for Medical Assistance to Travelers advises on illnesses and helps you locate English-speaking medical caregivers in other countries.  http://www.iamat.org

## Action Plan

### Personal response:
Discuss your personal medical concerns with your physician.
Get copies of your prescriptions.
Check your medical insurance coverage.

### Awareness:
How will your team obtain safe drinking water?
Create a team medical kit and select a team nurse or first aid person.

# Chapter 13

## Packing Pearls

### Mission Fashion Statement

Where you are going and what you are doing will determine, in part, what you will wear on a Short-Term Mission. Cultural considerations may also influence your choices. For example:

- When in a church, women may be expected to wear a hat, scarf or mantilla;
- In parts of Mexico and South America, open-toed shoes are inappropriate;
- In various countries, red, white, black, or purple clothing denote mourning;
- In many Moslem countries, women must wear scarves, long-sleeved shirts and pants, showing no skin except hands and face;
- Shorts and jeans, whether worn by men or women are not acceptable in most churches;
- In many cultures, bare midriff tops, low-cut and spaghetti-strapped shirts are not appropriate;
- In South Asia, women who wear their hair loose, are thought to be loose women;
- In many cultures throughout the world, women may not wear shorts (of any length).

## Jewelry

Leave jewelry at home. A simple wedding band and engagement ring and small stud earrings are fine in most situations, but flashy, large stones, expensive watches, bracelets, necklaces and earrings often attract the wrong attention, putting you and the team in jeopardy. If you need a watch, purchase an inexpensive one with a buckle strap which is more difficult to slip off the wrist in a snatch-and-run theft. Never leave jewelry out in the open in a hotel room; keep it in your locked suitcase or carry it with you.

## Party

About two weeks before the trip, hold a "packing party." Regulations concerning the size, shape and number of bags you may check or carry on a plane are changing as airlines tighten rules and try to increase their revenues. Check early in your planning and again right before you leave to be certain what you may do and what it may cost. For most of our years of mission travel, the maximum weight per checked bag has been fifty pounds. We weigh every bag before we go so there are no unpleasant surprises.

Early in your preparation, ask team members to plan to take one suitcase for their personal use and one for packing team supplies. At the packing party, have everyone bring a suitcase to fill with team supplies. Instruct them to intersperse some of their own clothing throughout the supplies to minimize problems going through Customs. For medical teams, you should also provide a letter (in the country's language) explaining why the team is bringing in medications and medical supplies. The sponsoring organization or the medical supply vendor can provide this letter. The letter is placed on top of the supplies in each suitcase.

Ask team members to list the supplies they are carrying and give you the list. Don't be surprised if something disappears during transit. With a master list, you can determine what is missing and whose luggage it had been in. If the medication or supply is the only one of its type and crucial to care, for example, a fetal stethoscope, pack it in the team medical kit or a carry-on bag.

A crucial multi-dose bottle of antibiotics disappeared from my checked bag on one trip. We changed our practice of bottling drugs at the clinic and began pre-bottling them so that if a few small bottles were stolen, the loss was not a disaster. Even then, on a recent trip a bag containing a large number of varied medications, and all of our alcohol wipes didn't make it to the clinic. We were, fortunately, able to replace the medications, but I had one very tense day trying to meet needs creatively until we could get new supplies.

You will also need an inventory or Bill of Laden for Customs officials of the country you are visiting. The Bill of Laden has the quantities and approximate value of each. Your host may require this ahead of time, but always carry a copy with you.

## Packing Tips

- Pack as much as possible in zippered-closure bags. Certainly any liquids, crayons, markers, glue, etc. need to be in bags, but also clothing because you can compress the bag and remove the air before zipping it closed. The bags are also handy in-country to keep dirty or wet clothing separate, hold trash until you can dispose of it, carry purchases (not every country has grocery bags), or conceal something you choose not to eat.

- Pack only what you absolutely must have, and what you can carry. Many places will not have elevators. Even getting on and off a bus with two or three suitcases is a challenge. Wearing the same clothes for more than one day may allow you to travel more comfortably with less baggage.

- Dress for comfort, not making a fashion statement. Be sure to break in new shoes before traveling. Check with your hosts about any clothing requirements or restrictions.

- Before you pack, look critically at your luggage. Are your suitcases sturdy and in good repair? Do the wheels and handles work properly? How easy would it be for someone to slice through the fabric? Do you have a tamper-proof luggage tag? You may wish to line the bottom of the suitcase with a large plastic trash bag so that if a hole develops, the contents are less likely to fall out. Duct tape works well to repair bags damaged during the trip.

- Be sure the team has identical, brightly-colored ties to mark every suitcase, including carry-on bags, for quick retrieval at the airport.

- Have one or two team members count luggage every time you transfer the suitcases.

## Carry-On Luggage

You are permitted to carry two bags (one suitcase, tote bag, or backpack and a smaller one such as a purse, computer case or briefcase) on the plane, but be sure to check with the airlines as this may change. Overhead space on planes can be limited and passengers are sometimes required to check carry-on bags before boarding. Since the items you are carry onto the plane are often crucial to your comfort and well-being or too valuable to let out of your sight, be sure you know whether you can part with a bag or redistribute certain items to another suitcase. Try to avoid the bulkhead seats which do not allow you to have your carry-on bag under a seat.

## What to Pack in a Carry-on Bag:

- Medications you must have daily or in an emergency, such as inhalers, insulin or an EpiPen®.
- An extra pair of glasses, or contacts. You may also want to have a copy of your lens prescription.
- Your camera and its case. Carrying a separate camera bag often attracts thieves.
- Whatever you need to make it through the night without your other bags should they not arrive.
- Your Passport, important papers, travelers' checks, money, copy of your Passport with extra photos, and team paperwork.
- A snack. You can't count on being fed on airplanes, or there may be unexpected delays during travel.
- Bottled water bought after going through security at the airport.

---

**The Big 5**
(Never be without)

- Your Passport
- Bottled water
- Toilet paper
- A bottle of alcohol gel
- A small flashlight

---

## Constant Companions

- Your **passport** is your identification, citizenship claim and ticket home. It cost a little more than $100 but it is worth several thousand dollars on the black market. Keep it with you at all times in a Passport holder or money belt worn beneath your clothing.

- **Bottled water** is often the only safe water for drinking, teeth brushing and washing. Check the seal of the cap before opening to be sure it isn't a used, refilled bottle.

- **Toilet paper** is not universally available. In many countries, the plumbing cannot handle paper waste. Use trash receptacles in restrooms or carry a plastic bag for disposal of paper.

- **Alcohol gel** is essential for cleaning your hands, especially if you have used water to wash them.

- A small **flashlight** can be a life-saver when there is a power outage, or in low-light situations.

---

Personal Experience

Imagine a small church in a rural village. The bathroom has three walls of concrete blocks surrounding a seatless toilet. The only light comes from the open doorway of the building twelve feet from the bathroom area. You can't see what might be inside or on the walls of the dark stall. If you needed to use the facilities, you'd be very glad you had a flashlight, toilet paper and alcohol gel with you.

---

## Team First Aid

In addition to you personal first-aid/medical kit, prepare a team first-aid kit which an assigned team member will carry at all times, including while traveling. The kit can fit into a small backpack or even a zippered lunch bag and then packed in a carry-on bag.

Team First Aid Kit

Aspirin, baby & enteric coated, acetaminophen, Ibuprofen
Digital thermometer with covers
Alcohol wipes
Cotton balls
Eye pads
Adhesive bandages of all sizes
Liquid Bandage®
Antibiotic ointment
Hydrocortisone cream
Finger and wrist splints
Ace wrap
Diphenhydramine HCl (Benadryl®)
Calamine lotion
Bismuth Subsalicylate (Pepto-Bismol®)
Anti-diarrheal medication
Laxative medication
Snake bite kit (optional)
Motion sickness or anti-nausea pills
Cough drops & throat lozenges
Vaseline
Temporary tooth glue
Eye drops, ear drops & nasal spray
Alcohol hand cleanser & hand wipes

## Don't Bring It Home

When we have an opportunity, we like to shop in a local grocery for candy or coffee or a local specialty such as hot sauce. These items are often less expensive than curios and convey the flavor of the culture as well as souvenirs. There are, however, items you should not bring home with you, including fresh fruit, vegetables, plants, flowers, animals, insects, fossils or bones.

Be very cautious when buying antiquities. What seems like an incredible find or bargain pottery may actually be a national treasure the government frowns on allowing out of the country.

## Personal Packing List

Passport, medical documents, copy of
passport and extra photos
Medications, copies of prescriptions,
personal medical supplies
Clothing, shoes, church-appropriate clothing,
jacket, sweat suit
Work gloves, hat, goggles, bandana or sweat
band
Spare batteries for flashlight, camera, or
hearing aid
Drinking cup
Cash for immediate needs or shopping
Flip-flops for shower (optional)
Rain poncho and folding umbrella
Unscented toiletries
Towel and washcloth
Bible, journal, pen or pencil
Travel or inflatable pillow (optional)
Camera (optional)
Alarm clock (optional)
Insect repellent and sunscreen
Snacks
Foreign language dictionary (optional)
Zippered closure bags and clothes pins
Photos of family or small photo album
Trash bags
Duct tape
Electrical power converter
Glasses, sunglasses, contact lenses & supplies

## Action Plan

### Personal response:
Create your own personal packing checklist.

### Awareness:
Schedule a Packing Party for the team.

### Making a Difference:
Plan for personal and team medical emergencies.
Prepare a team First Aid kit.

# Chapter 14

## Cross-Cultural Sensitivity

*We don't ask other cultures to change, but rather, <u>we</u> change so that they can receive the message of God.*

A Short-Term Mission always spans cultural boundaries, requiring preparation for the cross-cultural aspect as an integral part of planning for the mission.
Culture influences all that people are and all that they do, including:

- customs
- language
- ideas
- patterns
- rituals
- beliefs
- values
- religion
- laws
- behavior of a society
- family structure

When you interact with another culture, good-hearted desires to "make things right" have a place, but God calls Christians to do more. Go for the job you hope to accomplish, but, more importantly, for the love of Jesus you will share.

Because you cannot completely leave your own culture behind, you need to become aware of its impact and look for ways to bridge the gap between your culture and that of the people you will serve.

An old Sioux Indian prayer says: *"Oh Great Spirit, grant me the wisdom to walk in another's moccasins before I criticize or pass judgment."*

## Developing a Missions Mindset

God is the author of cultural sensitivity. He has a heart for people, and we must share in that loving concern. Understanding His character—that He knows and loves all people of all races and cultures—is the first step toward developing a cross-cultural, missions mindset.

A mindset is a set of beliefs, assumptions or methods which reinforce choices and behavior. All of us have some degree of cultural bias; we hold certain beliefs about people who are different from us.

Why should you be concerned with cultural differences? Culture determines both the message you share and the message others perceive.

*When the day of Pentecost came, they were
all together in one place. Suddenly a sound
like the blowing of a violent wind came from heaven
and filled the whole house where they
were sitting. They saw what seemed to be
tongues of fire that separated and came to rest
on each of them. All of them were filled with the*

*Holy Spirit and began to speak in other
tongues as the Spirit enabled them.*

*Now there were staying in Jerusalem*

*God-fearing Jews from every nation under heaven. When they heard this sound, a crowd came together in bewilderment, because each one heard them speaking in his own language.*

*Utterly amazed, they asked: "Are not all these men who are speaking Galileans? Then how is it that each of us hears them in his own native language? Parthians, Medes and Elamites; residents of Mesopotamia, Judea and Cappadocia, Pontus and Asia, Phrygia and Pamphylia, Egypt and the parts of Libya near Cyrene; visitors from Rome (both Jews and converts to Judaism); Cretans and Arabs- we hear them declaring the wonders of God in our own tongues!"*
Acts 2:1-11

The Holy Spirit did not change each person's ability to hear the words of the Apostles, but rather, the perception of the words so that the people heard the message in their own languages.

Beth Doerr, who works with ECHO, an organization whose goal is to equip people with resources and skills to reduce hunger and improve the lives of the poor, addressed the challenges of working cross-culturally. She asked, "Do we focus on what they don't have?"

Instead, she suggests that we consider their assets and strengths and use what they have to find answers. Finding opportunities changes the way people see themselves and their environment. She concluded, "A different point of view simply comes from being in a place where you are not."

148

# How to "Speak Another's Language"

Seek common grounds by:
- Sharing photos of your family
- Talking about your children or grandchildren

Make friendships:
- Address hosts by their titles until invited to use first names
- Learn the names of your hosts
- Wear name tags so that they can learn your names
- Bring a few extra nametags for your hosts so that they feel like a part of your team

Respect and embrace the richness of other cultures:
- Ask questions, research their customs, traditions, history and lifestyles
- Embrace differences and seek similarities
- Learn how to greet your hosts in their language or customs
- Learn how to say simple greetings, "please" and "thank you" in their language

Go as a learner:
- Ask them to teach you
- Be humble
- Resist the urge to think "your way" is the best or only way

Be quick to listen and slow to act:
- Time and timing vary from culture to culture, take a cue from your hosts

Maintain unity as a team:
- Work together and show respect to each other and your hosts

Suspend judgment; cultivate flexibility, adaptability:
- Establish "learning" and "serving" as the primary goals of team members

## Creating Bridges instead of Barriers

Understanding biases and prejudices helps to prepare the team for experiencing another culture during the Short-Term Mission. Discuss beliefs to increase the awareness of team members about the filters through which they assess others.    For example, ask team members what they think when they meet a mother with ten children living in poverty.

Do they believe:
- She is irresponsible for having children she cannot afford?
- She is unaware of birth control measures?
- She is fortunate to have been blessed by God with so many children?
- She might need to have children who will work the family farm or care for her in her old age?

Instead of applying our cultural standards to her life, think about her culture, lifestyle and beliefs.

## Examining Stereotypes

Stereotyping people causes biases and prejudices.  Ask team members to complete the following sentences:
All athletes are
All people on welfare are
All Americans are
All homosexuals are
All lawyers/politicians are
All people who sleep on grates are
All Christian Fundamentalists are
All male ballet dancers are
All Jewish mothers are
All construction workers are

Compare answers. Do their answers reflect any prejudice or bigotry? Next, discuss the characteristics of these groups of people:

African-Americans
Jews
Japanese
Liberals
Conservatives
Politicians
Hispanics
Republicans
Democrats
Athletes
Teachers
Cheerleaders
Men
Women
Rich people

What have you learned about your own biases?

We're not the only ones who stereotype others. People from around the world often describe Americans as loud, selfish, inconsiderate, always in a hurry, distant, materialistic and disrespectful of elders.

They also view us as having positive virtues such as a strong work ethic, promotion of individualism, belief in equality, and orientation to the future.

What behaviors would dispel the negative attributes and accentuate the positive?

## Developing a Plan

Now that the team is more aware of biases and the potential impact of prejudice, develop a plan for how you will handle cultural differences on the Short-Term Mission.

Education is a first step. Getting to know people from other cultures, reaching out to others in friendship, and focusing on commonality give opportunities to see them as God sees them. Focus on your love for Christ to break down racial, ethnic, cultural and economic barriers that can relationships. If you see poverty as arising from broken or distorted relationships, you will understand your role in missions as restoring relationships between people and between God and his children. Understanding basic cultural differences can also help.

* * *

We were traveling through small villages in the Yucatan Peninsula when we stopped to rest at a well in the center of a town. A young woman approached the well, anxious to fill a container she carried on her hip.

"Hola," my daughter said.

The woman bent to her task without returning the greeting.

We wanted to speak to her, to ask about her family, her village, and her life. After all, we had come to learn about the culture. What we did not understand was, she could not speak to us without the consent of her husband. We were strangers, outsiders, foreigners, even if we had come with friendly intentions.

* * *

## Communication Styles

Culture influences how people express themselves, to whom they talk, and how. Communication also includes the substance and manner of what is said (verbal), the timing, the emotional content, the distance between the speakers, and body language (nonverbal).

Even within a culture, there can be major differences in communication styles, especially between genders. My husband is a direct, to-the-point person, while I prefer to meander around the point as I relate all of the details of the entire story.

## Fundamental Cultural Differences

- Communication Styles
- Attitudes toward Conflict
- Conceptions of Time and Task Completion
- Self-Disclosure
- Information Acquisition

Communicating also involves more than what is spoken and what is heard. Gestures, body language and eye contact vary from person to person and culture to culture. These components can also easily cause misinterpretation of what is said and what is left unsaid.

---

Abuela and Grandmother

Many years ago, my family helped refugees who left Cuba when Castro came into power. One family with an elderly grandmother stayed in our home. At that time, my great-grandmother also lived with us. These two women, both in their eighties, did not seem to understand that they weren't speaking the same language.

One would say something to the other, and when the correct answer wasn't forth-coming, the statement would be repeated in a louder tone. Each thought the other had a hearing problem. Finally, they would be shouting at each other, until someone came along to translate.

---

Effective cross-cultural communication requires patience and perseverance. Interpreters can help, however, there is still the potential for mistranslation of the words, or misunderstanding of the non-spoken parts of communication. When you have a translator, be especially careful about using technical terms or jargon. Phrases such as "born in the Spirit," "share my testimony," "give witness," and "Vacation Bible School" can be difficult to understand and translate.

Learn about the gestures and body language of the host culture. Are there gestures they find offensive or embarrassing? For example, the "OK" sign Americans use is offensive in some other cultures. If asked how tall your child is, you might hold your hand up palm down at a certain height to indicate how tall she is compared to yourself. In Ecuador, the correct hand gesture is to turn the hand sideways. Doing it your way describes the height of an animal, and therefore, insults a person.

## Conflict Resolution

Individuals and cultures also have different ways to handle conflict. In the U.S., we usually encourage people to deal with conflict directly. In some cultures, conflict is viewed as embarrassing and demeaning, to be dealt with privately, possibly even with a written exchange rather than discussion. If there is conflict within the team, nip gossip in the bud, and encourage the participants to move to a private area to avoid drawing in others, or offending your hosts. Deal promptly with problems, and keep in mind, you only have one enemy.

*My prayer is not for them alone. I pray also for those who will believe in me through their message, that all of them may be one, Father, just as you are in me and I am in you. May they also be in us so that the world may believe that you have sent me. I have given them the glory that you gave me, that they may be one as we are one: I in them and you in me. May they be brought to complete unity to let the world know that you sent me*

*and have loved them even as you have loved me.*
John 17: 20-23

## Concepts of Time and Task Completion

There can be cultural differences regarding time and work. Our Western culture emphasizes time and task orientation, while other cultures focus more on relationships between people.

Since my husband is an engineer, we have enjoyed the friendship of an Ecuadorian engineer. Several years after our acquaintance, he told us how shocked he was to see my husband work alongside others on our construction teams. In his culture, an engineer supervises the laborers. It would not occur to him, nor would it be acceptable, to join in the work.

*Time is money* reflects our preference for structure and efficiency. We live by the clock, calendar and planner. Other cultures value other aspects of the job.

When we show up at a construction project site, we are often amazed that the local workers might not arrive at a specific starting time, that the supplies for the day's job might not be readily available, that everyone must have a hearty breakfast before they work, that there may not be a plan for what we are to do that day. Our concerns (and frustrations) come from our time-conscious, task-focused culture.

Other cultures have different expectations about time and task. For our Ecuadorian hosts, the value of relationships always comes before the job. Because we have learned this, we now spend a few minutes greeting everyone, shaking hands, inquiring about family, thanking them for coming, etc.

On a Short-Term Mission, flexibility and allowing "their way" to be the best way are the keys to getting the job done.

155

## Self-Disclosure

In some cultures, disclosing personal information is also taboo. This can be a unique problem for a medical team. Additionally, there may be cultural issues with a male doctor providing care for females. You may need to be prepared for a female nurse to perform examinations with the physician's hands-off supervision. Ask in advance about attitudes and practices in the culture and location where you will work.

## Information Acquisition

Our culture values learning in formal settings, in schools, and from books. We respect authorities and experts. Other cultures place greater emphasis on knowledge gained through experience, tradition, and age.

One of the highlights of my mission trips came when a woman requested a house call for her father who was too ill to walk to the clinic. Three of us visited him. He had arthritis and catarracts, and all we could offer him were a few pain pills. His wife, a Quechua healing woman, gave us a tour of her garden, explaining the medicinal plants she grew. With her knowledge of herbs, and her garden, she could actually treat his ailments far better than we could.

Respect the wisdom and ways of others, even when they differ, or seem "less advanced" than yours.

The language of mothering is the same throughout the world. Speaking one mother to another has value for both cultures. I marvel at the diversity in raising children, yet the unity in how we all care for our children and want what is best for them. Whenever an opportunity arises, I praise mothers for how they interact with their babies and mother them. Every mother, no matter where she lives, needs a word of encouragement.

## Cross-Cultural Pitfalls:
## Food, Fashion and Photos

Food/drink are highly symbolic in many cultures. If you reject food, not only do you rebuff an offer of friendship, but you may also be giving the message that their food isn't good enough for you.
Accept their gifts of food and drink gratefully, even if you don't think you can eat or drink it. Unless you have some health or dietary restriction, try it. You might be surprised that you enjoy it. If you do need to decline, don't offer an excuse of a food allergy, simply ask if you might save it to enjoy later. (This is where a zippered-closure bag comes in handy.)

Your hosts may have provided a special food at great cost to them. In Ecuador, guinea pig is an expensive delicacy. Because we know that the team will be offered a roasted guinea pig which, by the way, is cooked and served whole, we prepare everyone so that their facial gestures and comments are appropriate.

Inappropriate dress can also offend your hosts. In many other cultures, women dress more conservatively and less casually. Shorts, bare midriffs, two-piece swimsuits, or open-toed shoes may not be acceptable. Ask your hosts in advance what clothing is appropriate and what situations might require special consideration. Many churches, for example, do not allow men or women in shorts to enter.

Avoid shirts and baseball caps with messages written on them. Even when they aren't offensive, the words may have entirely different meanings in another language. For example, the word "nova" means a bright star to us, but it is "no go" in Spanish.

Men should always remove hats when entering buildings, especially churches, and women may need to wear something on their heads in some churches.

Be sensitive with your camera. In some areas, especially public places such as a market, you may be expected to pay for a photo. Always ask permission before taking someone's picture. Be careful about taking photos of military installations or personnel, or government buildings.

Your team might think of a mission trip in terms of their own effort, their investment of time, talent and money. Instead, consider focusing on God's role. You do not go "on your own," but you go with God, as His ambassadors and servants.

Ambassadors represent their country, culture and people with the authority of their government. An ambassador acknowledges the sovereignty of the government, culture and tries to foster a relationship of mutual respect by seeking common goals.

A servant lays down control of the future on a day-to-day basis to put another's needs and wants ahead of self. A servant looks for ways to enhance life.

A missionary is one who is sent by God to represent Him, who goes willingly to share the love of God with others. Not by our own power, but with the authority and blessing of God.

## Culture Shock

When a person visits a culture that is very different, "culture shock" may result, causing feelings of homesickness, irritability, anger, frustration, discouragement, disorientation, and alienation. These emotions can produce negative behavior such as: complaining, criticism, obsession with health/illness, preoccupation with cleanliness, withdrawal, and increased need for sleep.

Travel often involves different time zones, food, sleep patterns and physical demands. Add in the emotional and psychological impact of the introduction to a new and different culture, and stress escalates. Be sure team members are eating, drinking sufficient water, resting, and sleeping on as normal a schedule as possible.

Preparing team members for these physical and emotional demands will help them process their experiences. Poverty can overwhelm even the most experienced team members. Cross-cultural training can prepare team members for the differences between cultures, prevent inadvertent cultural blunders, and promote global perspectives. However, even with the most thorough training, encountering the level of poverty common in the Developing World can produce an emotional response (culture shock) similar to the stages of grief.

## Responses

1. Denial—the mind's attempt to prevent emotional overload. Denial may present as withdrawal, disconnection, isolation, or anxiety and fears.
2. Anger—often combines with frustration, hurt, disappointment, fear or outrage. Anger asks: "How can people live like this?"
3. Bargaining—moving from anger into questioning: "Why would a loving God allow this to happen?"
4. Depression—including guilt. Depression asks: "Why do I have so much, and they have so little?"
5. Acceptance occurs when you acknowledge your emotional response to the problems and move toward investigating solutions: "I cannot be all things to all people, but I can do what God enables me to do in this situation."

During one trip, the team visited a small village of five or six one-room huts with no electricity or source of clean water. A crowd of children ran out to greet us. Their parents had to leave them throughout the week to work in a nearby city. An elderly woman provided the only adult supervision for the twenty-five or so little ones. We walked around the area, noting the empty

159

one-room school that had no teacher, the empty soccer field that had no ball, the dirty pond down the side of the mountain, their only source of water.

That evening, as the team gathered to discuss their impressions of the day, one woman summed up her whole experience with one sentence, "The children didn't have shoes."

Shoes were the last thing most people would have noticed in a place without electricity, clean water, food, parents, education, medical care, safe and comfortable housing. We realized then the necessity of daily meetings with the team members to process their observations and experiences.

A time of daily de-briefing is essential to help the team cope with feelings, experiences and attitudes. Plan to meet daily, either in the morning to discuss and prepare the day or in the evening to recap and plan for the next day.

A daily de-briefing might begin with a simple question, such as: "What was the high point and low point of your day?" You might ask, "How did the day meet or not meet your expectations?" or "What was different than your expectations?"

Allow each person a few minutes to think and answer. Go around the group and be sure everyone has an opportunity to speak. Sharing the same answer is fine, but not talking at all can be a signal that the person is having trouble assimilating the experiences. Talking about expectations versus reality helps put the experiences of the day into context.

There are often days that hit someone hard. The wise leader prepares in advance by getting to know the team members, but you cannot always know what will affect others or how they will process an experience.

\* \* \*

## A Day of Drama

Early in the week, we had a very difficult day in the clinic with two nurses becoming upset and tearful as they worked with a child who revealed that she was being sexually abused. Both nurses had had personal experience with this.

Most of the team knew something was going on, but not what. When we got together that evening for debriefing, I wanted to explain what had happened in a way that would be sensitive to the nurses, and try to keep the emotions leftover from the morning from taking over the meeting.

Instead of asking our usual "high and low points" questions, I began the meeting with a simple statement acknowledging the drama of the day. I explained what had happened and how the situation had been handled with a great deal of sensitivity and prayer. We kept the evening as low-key as possible, shared a few more tissues and prayed together as a group.

By not keeping to our usual de-brief discussion, we helped everyone work through a difficult experience.

\* \* \*

Daily de-briefs also begin to consider how team members will respond when they return home and are asked, "So, how was the trip?"

It is so easy to answer, "Great!" or "You should go" or "It was a life-changing experience." While the answers are genuine and heartfelt, they don't tell anyone anything. And when you try to explain how it was life-changing, your words sometimes sound hollow or fall flat. The person who asked wasn't there with you and often doesn't "get" what you're saying because the life-changing part happened within your heart, not his.

By talking about the highs and lows, the expectations and realities, team members learn how the experiences are affecting them, what lessons God is teaching them, exactly how their lives are being changes, and often, how they will respond both to the questions others will ask and to the burdens God is putting on them now.

On the last night of the trip, we always ask team members, "How will you respond when someone asks about your trip?"

We help them frame responses that show how God worked in their lives and the lives of those they met. We try to move them from telling to showing how God touched their hearts.

* * *

*May the God who gives endurance and encouragement give you a spirit of unity among yourselves as you follow Christ Jesus, so that with one heart and mouth you may glorify the God and Father of our Lord Jesus Christ.*

*Accept one another, then, just as Christ accepted you, in order to bring praise to God.*
*For I tell you that Christ has become a servant of the Jew on behalf of God's truth, to confirm the promises made to the patriarchs.*
Romans 15: 5-8

## Action Plan

### Personal response:
Look forward to the experience of a lifetime, meeting new friends, sharing unique Christian fellowship, and rejoicing in the diversity of God's people.

### Awareness:
Learn how to greet and respond to greetings in your host's language.
Take time with greetings and good-byes; follow the lead of the hosts.
Include your hosts in group prayers and team activities.

### Making a Difference:
Prepare the team for a cross-cultural experience.
Make a plan for team de-briefing.

# Chapter 15

## Poverty

*What does the Lord require of you?*
*To act justly and to love mercy*
*and to walk humbly with your God.*
Micah 6:8

### "You Will Always Have the Poor"

You can't miss this message. These words of Jesus are recorded in three of the four Gospels. I used to think he was somehow giving us permission to ignore the poor, after all, they had been present before, during and after his lifetime. They would *always* be there, a regular feature of life on earth, like wars, famine and disease.

I experienced disconnection because I could not truly identify with the poor, and yet, I wanted to help in some way. My family participated in the CROP Walk to raise money to alleviate world hunger. We worked occasionally at a local soup kitchen, and gave used clothing to those in need. We sponsored a child from another country and sent money every month. We gave when there was a natural disaster anywhere in the world. With all of these activities, I felt comfortable that I was doing my part.

But I still really knew nothing about poverty.

In my work as a homecare nurse, I have visited patients in the poorer sections of town. I had traveled through slums in other countries. Yet coming face to face with poverty still did not have the effect of seeing it in the faces of children. The children of Rio Verde started me down the path of learning the meaning of being poor in a Developing Country.

## Nancy's Story

Nancy was a nine-year-old child, several years older than six years of age I'd have guessed from her diminuitive size. She had responsibility for the toddler in her arms, and two other siblings. A baby brother had died recently from dehydration brought on by diarrhea. Her mother had to leave their home on Monday to work in the city and could not return until the end of the week. No one knew about a father.

Six families, including Nancy's, lived in a squatters' village of cardboard and scrap tin huts on the side of a mountain. All of the adults except an elderly couple travelled weekly to a large city for work, leaving behind twenty-eight children to fend for themselves. The village had a school, a one-room building with a few benches and tables, and a scarred, old chalkboard. No paper, pencils, crayons, books, toys, computers, or teachers.

When I met Nancy, she and her siblings were coming to a church camp three days a week for a meal. Each child brought a metal or plastic dish and a cup. Nancy balanced the three-year-old on her lap, making certain he ate his soup, rice and a piece of bread. Then, she ate what remained of his lunch. Her own portion of food went into her bowl to be saved for the next day. If she was careful, her three meals would feed the family all week until their mother returned on Saturday. Of course, she had no refrigeration for the soup, pieces of chicken and rice. And, no way to keep insects, vermin, animals or other people from getting the food.

The story has no happy ending. I don't know what has happened in Nancy's life. God used her in my life, as I hope He is using me in the lives of children like her. At the beginning of my journey in learning and serving, she pushed me to begin examining my own life and responsibility to others.

## What is Poverty?

It is difficult to examine poverty without politicizing it, without finger-pointing, without feeling helpless, or even guilty. After all, we are a culture who "pulls ourselves up by our bootstraps." We expect each generation to be better off than the preceding one. We expect most people to reach their full potentials and lead creative, productive lives. We accept these conditions as the norm and don't really comprehend that the majority of the world's people and nations live below the U.N. poverty level of less than $2 (USD) per day.

According to Ron Tschetter, the former director of the Peace Corps, one billion people worldwide live on less than $1 per day. Two-three billion people go to bed hungry every night.

Poverty is defined as a state or condition of having little money, goods or means of support. Poverty involves more than the absence of material wealth. Poverty also includes the inability to meet basic human needs for food, safe water, shelter, clothing, healthcare and education. Poverty comes from a lack of options, resources, skills and knowledge, and the inability to exert influence or access social power. A root cause of poverty is often injustice.

Poverty involves being trapped in a condition of vulnerability and powerlessness. Poverty can be generational, in which two or more generations are born into this environment, or situational, resulting from loss associated with some event. For example, when a natural disaster destroys all possessions and the ability to recover from the disaster, a family can be pushed from a precarious place into poverty.

Children born into generational poverty rarely have the tools and ability to escape. Persons coping with situational poverty may or may not be able to recover.

Some experts blame external forces such as natural disasters, while others look to internal reasons such as ignorance and apathy.

## Causes and Contributors of Poverty

- Warfare, civil unrest, and government repression
- Agricultural cycles, droughts, floods and natural disasters
- Environmental degradation
- Overpopulation
- Unequal distribution of resources, and lack of basic infrastructure to move resources
- Ignorance and inadequate education
- Lack of employment opportunities
- Colonialism and slavery
- Apathy, lack of personal commitment, laziness
- Disease, illness, malnutrition and poor health
- Dishonesty, political corruption and injustice
- Dependency, especially multi-generational
- Life choices
- Hopelessness, disengagement, and immobility
- Skewed perception of reality, preconceived ideas, and poverty mentality
- Fatalism that accepts the way things have always been
- Transfer of responsibility to others, excuses
- Fear and desperation

## What Can Be Done?

Poverty is not only widespread globally, but its causes overwhelm the organizations and agencies dedicated to trying to alleviate it. Members of the United Nations adopted the Millennium Declaration which established these anti-poverty directives, to be met by 2015:

- Eradicate extreme poverty and hunger;
- Achieve universal primary education;
- Promote gender equality and empower women;
- Reduce child mortality;
- Improve maternal health;
- Combat HIV/AIDS, malaria and other diseases;
- Ensure environmental sustainability;
- Develop global partnership for development.

These programs do not, however, address the mentality of poverty. Eradicating poverty requires that people find, or create opportunities to change how they see themselves and their environment. The root cause of poverty is broken or distorted relationships.

- The relationship between people and God
- The relationship between people
- The relationship between a person's body, spirit, emotions and mind
- The relationship between people and their environment

Mother Teresa of Calcutta understood the role of the physical, emotional and spiritual aspects of life. She wrote:

*"When I pick up a person from the street, hungry, I give him a plate of rice, a piece of bread, I am satisfied. I have removed that hunger. But a person that is shut out, that feels unwanted, unloved, terrified, the person that has been thrown out from society*
*–that poverty is so hurtable [sic] and so much, and I find that very difficult."*

# What Can One Person Do?

Perhaps you are like me, overwhelmed by the magnitude of poverty. I certainly can't stop wars, affect agricultural cycles, droughts, floods or natural disasters. I cannot pull the economy out of recession. My own city has issues with infrastructure. I'm not even sure I know what environmental sustainability is. What can I do about ignorance, apathy, dishonesty and dependence?

The American author Edward Everett Hale offered this answer: "I am only one, but I am one. I cannot do everything, but I can do something. And I will not let what I cannot do interfere with what I can do."

# Doing Something

Educate yourself. Learn about poverty: where it is, what it is, and why it exists. Look beyond the statistics that are impossible to fully comprehend. Find one issue which interests you: homelessness, hunger, clean water, healthcare, education, HIV/AIDS, indoor air pollution from wood fires, gardening and food-production, education or the empowerment of women. Research and find a way to put your passion for the topic to work for someone else.

> *"Like Jesus, we belong to the world, living not for ourselves, but for others."*
> Mother Teresa

Make a difference in one person's life. Sponsor a child from another country. Introduce your own family to the poverty issues you are examining. Volunteer at a soup kitchen or on a Habitat for Humanity project. Tutor an immigrant in English or help someone learn to read. Join or lead a Short-Term Mission Team.

# Who Am I that I Should Go?

*If you can't feed a hundred people, then feed just one.*
Mother Teresa

Offer a hand-up rather than a handout. You cannot alleviate poverty by attacking its symptoms. Teaching people, empowering women, improving health, seeding business ventures, creating opportunities for employment, and most important of all, giving hope for a better future will eradicate poverty.

A Short-Term Mission project is an ideal vehicle for alleviating the suffering of God's people. When you leave your own comfort zone to meet people at their level, in their environment, in their needs, you give a powerful message of hope and love. Education, training and empowerment are the avenues out of the cycle of poverty. A mission project is an intentional act of reconciliation, reaching out one person at a time to restore relationships between one person to another, one person to their environment or one person to God..

*We can do no great things, only*
*small things with great love.*
Mother Teresa

Seek God's answers to the problems of poverty. Sarah Corson, a career missionary and co-founder of the mission organization, Servants in Faith and Technology, shared this story. As she and her family traveled in the back of a truck from their village to a larger city, they came upon a truck going in the opposite direction. Both vehicles were stuck, and Sarah began to converse with a young woman sitting in the bed of the other truck. She had taken her family's farm produce to the city to sell it, and in the process of traveling there and back, she had not had anything to eat for a day.

Sarah had sandwiches for her family and she offered one to the woman. However, when Sarah tossed the bag with the sandwich to the woman, one of the trucks suddenly started up again and the sandwich fell to the mud between the trucks.

The woman smiled and called out her thanks as they separated.

Why was the woman grateful when her hunger had not been satisfied?

Someone had cared enough to share from her own meager supplies, and even though Sarah was unable to meet the woman's physical need, she felt blessed.

## "Act Justly"

I must confess I have never understood the "Peace and Justice" movement in some churches. Because I thought that poverty was supposed to exist, I didn't recognize the role of justice in poverty. And I certainly didn't accept that an ordinary person would have any responsibility in supporting justice. Peace and Justice seemed liked governmental issues. The last time I participated in anything remotely related was during my college years when I demonstrated against the Viet Nam War (and was tear-gassed for it).

Recently, our pastor taught for several Sundays on the passage from Micah quoted at the beginning of this chapter. He suggested that "to do justice" means to be concerned with the needs of others and to do something about it.

That made sense to me. The pastor went on to suggest that doing justice begins with worshipping God, being obedient and giving fully of oneself to Him. Love God, love others, serve both.

Justice requires obedience to God's laws, living in line with God's character. Justice encourages responsibility to others.

*The righteous care about justice for the poor.*
Proverbs 29:7

When we practice justice we value people as God does. We respect their differences and defend them. We try to meet their needs. Dealing with poverty then becomes a personal commitment to God's people and to justice for them. Justice requires us to see people's needs. Mercy enables us to act on needs.

*Give yourself fully to God. He will use you to accomplish great things on the condition that you believe much more in His love than in your own weakness.*
Mother Teresa

Foster in yourself and others the understanding of God's role expressed in human efforts which, along with the resources He supplies, can become the answer to poverty. Even though we as a people are richly blessed, God's resources are not limited to us.

The challenge of working in missions is often helping others identify their blessings. When we change our focus from what people do not have to what they do have, we help them embrace their role in improving their situation.

\* \* \*

In the *Universal Declaration of Human Rights* (1948), the United Nations established, "Everyone has the right to work, to just and favorable conditions of work and to protection for himself and his family [and] an existence worthy of human dignity ... Everyone has the right to a standard of living adequate for the health and well-being of himself and his family, including food, clothing, housing and medical care."

The U.N. goes on to say that meeting basic human needs requires:

- A stable political, social and economic environment, with related freedoms, such as ownership of land and property;

- the ability to make free and educated choices;

- participation in a democratic environment in which one can determine one's own future.

This bears repeating, study and prayer:

> *What does the Lord require of you?*
> *To act justly and to love mercy*
> *and to walk humbly with your God.*
> Micah 6:8

* * *

*But the plans of the Lord stand firm forever, the purposes*
*of his heart through all generations. From heaven the*
*Lord looks down and sees all mankind; from his*
*dwelling place he watches all who live on earth-*
*he who forms the hearts of all who considers*
*everything they do.*
Psalms 33: 11, 13-15

## Action Plan

### Personal response:
Make a personal commitment to learn about poverty.
Find and research a poverty issue that interests you.

### Awareness:
Discuss how your team can and will alleviate the suffering
of God's people.

### Making a Difference:
Prepare your team for their encounter with poverty by
discussing poverty, its
causes and how one person can make a difference.

Who Am I that I Should Go?

# Chapter 16

## STM: Spiritual Growth

*"The joy of the Lord is your strength"*
*Nehemiah 8:10*

Short-Term Missions are an excellent vehicle for spiritual growth, a life-long journey of getting to know Christ, and becoming more like him.

Participating in Short-Term Missions involves two basic beliefs:

- God has a heart for *all* people;

- God chooses to work through people, as inefficient as we are, to fulfill His plan.

Our culture wants positive messages, achievement, success, and wealth, but what our society preaches and what God says don't always match. On a Short-Term Mission, you leave your comfort zone, utilizing your own resources of time and money, to go into harm's way for people you may not even know. Jesus' "riches to rags" story offers the model of servanthood.

Christ challenges each person to commit to serving others by giving all that we *have* to all that we *know* Christ to be. Servanthood is an act of obedience to God's purpose, and the answer to Christ's command to go into the world and make disciples of all people. God's intention for us is to love one another and to be a witness for Christ by performing our ministry where we have been called to do it.

*I tell you the truth, anyone who has faith in me will do what I have been doing. He will do even greater things than these because I am going to the Father.*
John 14: 12, 13

God works in each of us in different ways. My journey is not the same as yours, just as we have different relationships with God. Scripture tells us:

*For this very reason, make every effort to add to your faith, goodness; and to goodness, knowledge; and to knowledge, self-control; and to self-control, perseverance; and to perseverance, godliness; and to godliness, brotherly kindness; and to brotherly kindness, love.*

*For if you possess these qualities in increasing measure, they will keep you from being ineffective and unproductive in your knowledge of our Lord Jesus Christ.*
2 Peter 1: 5-8

## The Source of Spiritual Growth

We often speak of the mountains and valleys in a journey of faith. But do you really understand what the analogy means? A simple explanation has the mountaintops being times of joy and great spiritual growth, while the valleys can be times of challenge to faith, doubt and defeat.

Driving on the team bus throughout Ecuador taught me about the true meaning of mountains and valleys in our faith journey, and what lies between the mountains and valleys.

When you travel down a mountainside, the going is quick and easy, and you can fall into the trap of forgetfulness and complacency. Life is sometimes comfortable and lulls you into expecting each day to be like the last. The status quo reigns in your life.

You reach the valley still in the sunshine of the afternoon, enjoying a relaxed pace as you cruise through life. But, ahead, the sun begins to slip behind the next mountain. Shadows gather in your path, quickening your steps as you recognize it's time to move on.

The climb requires more energy, perseverance, and more trust than you think you have. The sun is gone now, the way is treacherous and arduous, full of switchbacks as you zigzag up. And you are growing tired. Perhaps you make the mistake of looking back. Rather than admiring the distance you have come, you see the sun still on the mountainside behind you and feel nostalgic envy about what was, what you've left.

The mountain of your doubts looms ahead and fear towers over your path. You want to give up, to return to the easier road. You forget the mountaintop experience of exhilaration from previous mountaintops. You can barely see the path as you put one foot in front of the other.

The mountaintops of life are brief, just long enough to inspire you to continue the journey. The valleys are short as well, just enough to lull you into lingering. The downs and ups of the mountain slopes are where the real growth, learning and work take place. The journey, every step of your path, is the source of your spiritual growth.

We don't need to concentrate on discovering God's will for our lives, but doing what we already know is God's will.

*And I will ask the Father, and he will give you another Counselor to be with you forever—the Spirit of truth. The world cannot accept him, because it neither sees him nor knows him. But you know him, for he lives with you and will be in you.*
John 14: 16, 17

## The Battleground

Will you always have the perfect team, wonderful spiritual experience, mission-accomplished project? Or, will you ever have the perfect team, wonderful spiritual experience and mission-accomplished team?

The single most important attitude every mission leader and team member needs is flexibility, and there is a good reason for that. Mission teams are fodder for the enemy's desire to wage war against God's kingdom. I would be remiss if I did not mention spiritual warfare. It is normal to experience doubts, fears, and worries while you are preparing a team. It is normal to experience dissension, grumbling, and assorted difficulties with a team. It is normal to have transportation woes, money problems, sickness, supply concerns, missed deadlines, project failures, and disappointment.

When we returned from one trip, we had a three-hour drive from the airport to our home city. We decided to stop for a meal and when I entered the restaurant to secure seating, I couldn't decide whether to ask for two tables of seven or seven tables of two each.

There has been more than one occasion when I pledged I would never lead another team. However, God always has other plans. The year after our most difficult and challenging mission, we had one of great peace and healing.

Spiritual growth, whether within you or in the team, is never easy. It reminds me of going to the gym where my trainer will give me more weight than I want to lift and expect me to lift it more times than I want to, so that I can tear muscles cells apart a little at a time and grow stronger over months (and years) of workouts. That's the way a mission team works. God demands more and more of you, because He can and He knows what will make you become the person He wants you to be.

Keep your eye on the prize, rather than the race, as Paul reminds us. And what a prize it is!

*But the fruit of the Spirit is love, joy, peace, patience, kindness, goodness, faithfulness, gentleness and self-control. Against such things there is no law.*
Galatians 5: 22, 23

## Scripture's Directives for a Team

Be prepared to:

- Encourage others (Romans 15:2)

- Accept others (Romans 15:7)

- Instruct others (Romans 15:14

- Pray for others (James 5:16)

- Carry each other's burdens (Galatians 6:2)

- Bear with others' failings (Romans 15:1)

\* \* \*

Almost 400 years ago, two small ships carried several hundred people from England to the Maryland colony. The boats bobbed on the Atlantic Ocean for six months, carried on the currents, pushed by winds until they landed on a distant shore. There, the people planted a way of life, religion, culture, government, households and families.

God is sending you into another culture, perhaps to another country. You take who you are with you wherever you go. Become all that God wants you to be. A Short-Term Mission team provides many opportunities for spiritual growth. Seek ways to enhance the experience for yourself and your team.

Invite team members to pray for the people you are serving and the team. An easy and non-threatening way to do this is to ask each person to rotate saying grace before your meals. Most people who would never feel comfortable praying aloud will say a prayer before eating.

For the first several years, our team members were primarily from the same church. We often held a Bible study during our preparatory meetings, and team members provided devotionals at mealtimes and evening de-briefings during the mission trip.

When we began recruiting medical teams, the composition of the teams changed because our church did not have a sufficient number of medical personnel to put together a team. Our medical teams came from different churches, religious backgrounds, and communities, making it more challenging to get everyone together for regular meetings. We have continued the custom of asking team members to pray before meals, and to present devotionals during evening de-briefings.

## The Importance of Prayer

*The presence of God is uniquely realized, and the*
*power of God is dramatically released when*
*God's people unite in prayer.*
Rev. Tom Walker

There is a spiritual battle for the hearts of people, and whether we are sharing God's love in words or deeds, we can be subject to attacks by Satan. Prayer is both necessary and vital because of the work the Short-term Mission does for the kingdom of God. Prayer is an integral part of a STM. Ask your team members to recruit prayer partners as well as financial supporters. Seek prayers to help prepare your hearts and the hearts of the people you will serve. Ask for prayer cover for safety and protection while you travel and work.

## Personal Stories

My mother and I lived in the same town, and I had been caring for her through several illnesses. She became gravely ill just prior to one of my STM trips. I agonized about what to do about my responsibility to her and to my team. The dilemma of whether to leave or stay with my mother allowed my four sisters to step in. They arranged to take turns coming to care for her so that I could go, but still, the decision to leave was very difficult and emotional.

A week after my return, my mother died. At first, I felt a great deal of guilt for having left. However, I now realize that my decision to go gave each of my sisters precious time with mother that they would not have had if I had stayed home.

A more difficult experience for us to understand was the unexpected death of the son of two team members. He had an accident while his parents were on a mission trip. Trying to reconcile the positives from our trip with the tragedy of their loss of a child challenged the faith of the whole team.

At times like that, we must choose to refocus. I recalled with the team the message I had shared during a worship service the week before. I had told our Ecuadorian brothers and sisters that life is not easy, not their lives, nor ours, but we all are looking forward to a life that is perfect and glorious when we join Christ in heaven.

Their son's death didn't change all of the good that Dave and Carmen accomplished on the STM. It didn't alter the work God was doing in the hearts and lives of the team and the people we serve.

The following year, Dave and Carmen were the first to join the next team, and asked if they could bring their daughter, a sister and brother-in-law, a dental assistant from his office, and a life-

182

long friend.  God continued to move even through this tragedy.

# Commissioning Ceremony

If possible, arrange for a Commissioning Ceremony or send-off for the team shortly before your scheduled trip. Involving the host church helps others understand and experience their roles as senders and supporters. Prayer and blessing commit the congregation to support the team, the purpose and goals of the project.

Choose a Bible story that reflects an inheritance of responsibility, such as 2 Kings 2: 8-15 which recounts the story of Elijah's passing his mantel to Elisha.  The mantel represents leadership, and reminds us that, on the mission field, others have come before us and others will follow.  During the mission, you are chosen servants of God, wearing the mantel of servants.

During the most memorable Commissioning Service for one of our teams, the pastor laid a white hand towel on each person's shoulder to represent the servanthood of Christ as he knelt to wash the feet of his apostles.  He encouraged the team members to find some way to use the towel to serve someone during the mission.

For another service, the pastor lit a candle for each team member, recalling that Jesus is the light of the world.  The congregation pledged to "leave the lights on" until the team returned.

## Sample Service of Sending Forth

In the Book of Acts, Chapter 1, Verse 8, Jesus says to his followers: "You will receive power when the Holy Spirit comes on you and you will be my witnesses in Jerusalem and in Judea and Samaria and to the ends of the earth."

# Who Am I that I Should Go?

Mission work is not a task for individuals. You are sent out together so that together, gathered by the Lord, you can make Him present in the world. As you prepare to leave, remember that you have with you the Holy Spirit to empower, to protect and to inspire you. Remember that we send you with love and prayers and support. Remember that Christ has chosen you to make known the Good News of salvation and the Glory of God.

Jesus Christ sent his followers into the world to bear witness to the coming of the Kingdom of God, and to serve others. Their loving witness and that of all who succeeded them still challenges us today. These team members who stand before us today continue that tradition. We send them forth in the name of Christ to serve and to witness.

(To the team): Do you, as mission team volunteers, promise you will be faithful servants of Jesus Christ? Will you support the goals and purpose of the mission project? Will you serve others so that by your work and your presence Jesus Christ will be glorified? Will you represent this church faithfully?

(To congregation): Do you, the members of this congregation promise to support these persons through your prayers for the success of their mission, and for their safety while they are traveling and working?

Let us pray: Father, we ask for your blessing on this team. Empower them to witness and serve as the Holy Spirit empowered the apostles. Protect them as they travel, learn and serve. Encourage and inspire them to witness with joy. Return them safely to us. We ask this in the name of your Son, Jesus Christ. May God richly bless and keep you on your mission. Amen

\* \* \*

*"You will receive power when the Holy Spirit comes on you; and you will be my witnesses in Jerusalem, and in all Judea and Samaria, and to the ends of the earth."*

Acts 1: 8

## Action Plan

### Personal response:
Consider the spiritual growth of your team.  Will you
Have Bible Study, prayer, and devotionals during
meetings as well as on the mission trip?

### Awareness:
Be aware of and address the spiritual needs of your
team members.

### Making a Difference:
Pray and enlist others in prayer for your team and
for the people you will serve.

# Chapter 17

## Sharing Your Story

*"Greater love has no one than this: to lay down one's life for one's friends. You are my friends if you do what I command. I no longer call you servants, because a servant does not know his master's business. Instead, I have called you friends, for everything that I learned from my Father I have made known to you."*
John 15: 13-15

Perhaps you've heard someone speak in your church, sharing a personal "testimony." Sometimes the person starts with describing how horrible he was before Christ came into his life. The encounter with Christ changed him in a profound way. Now his life is better because of God. The message is meant to inspire and encourage the audience.

Going on a mission trip, you might be asked to share your story with the people you meet, or with your church when you return. But, what if that thought terrifies you? You didn't have some life-changing event that converted you. You've been going to church all your life and your relationship with God is a private conviction you don't know how to share with others. You might even think your story is boring.

The Good News we're supposed to share with others doesn't have to begin with the bad news of your life before you met

186

Christ. Sharing your personal story of faith in another culture requires the additional consideration of relating to people who may not understand your history, heritage and culture. How could I explain coming to know Christ at a small group Bible study in my dorm to people who have no idea what dorm life is like or what goes on in a small group study?

A simple and effective way to share your faith begins with who you are and how you are just like the people to whom you are speaking. Tell them you are a wife, or husband, mother or father or grandparent. Talk about the challenges of relating to the people in your family, of raising children in today's world. Focus on your commonalities. Married couples want to know how to live out their lives and marriage in God's will. Every parent wants to raise children who love God and obey Him.

I like to ask if the women in the room remember the precious time of expecting a baby and how much they loved that baby even before they met the child. God loves us even before we know Him. Then, as our child grows up, he may do something we don't like. We learn that we can still love the child without liking what he's doing. Likewise, God loves us even when we don't do what is right. He opens His arms to take us back when we ask for His forgiveness.

Woman-to-woman, mother-to-mother, person-to-person sharing tells the story of how God acts in your life in a way that other persons can relate to and apply to their own lives.

Talk to others as if they are your friends. To this point I have described a mission project as an exercise in servanthood. When Jesus Christ, however, spoke to his disciples, he moved them from being servants to friends. As you serve others, you are putting aside your own desires and life in order to become friends in Christ's name.

To prepare your own life story, ask yourself these questions:
- Who am I?

- How am I like the persons with whom I want to share my story?
- What similarities can I use to relate to them?
- How is God working in my life today?
- How might He be working in their lives as well?
- What lessons has He taught me that might apply to others' lives?

When you share your story, try to avoid using "church jargon." A translator might not be familiar with words such as "testimony," "rebirth," "born again," and so on. Even if the words are translatable, they might not make sense to the listeners. When using a translator, speak slowly and pause after every couple of sentences to allow translation. Observe the listeners' faces to be certain they understand what you have been saying.

## Coming Home

You've come home now from your mission trip and want to share it with others. You want to tell someone, anyone, about your experiences. Something remarkable, perhaps even life-changing has happened, and you have to share the story. You've spent a week with a wonderful group of people, but they've all gone home, back to their lives. Who will you talk to? Who will understand what you've been through? How will you share the story of what you saw and did, of the people whose lives you touched, and of the change within you? How many photos do you have to show? What will you do next? How will you deal with God? How will He deal with you?

## Debriefing

Daily debriefing during the Short-Term Mission helps team members learn how to incorporate the experiences of the STM into their lives, and how to share them with others. Evening discussions with questions about what has transpired throughout the day encourage team members to learn how to share their experiences when they return home. On the last night before going home, ask how the project has changed them, and what they will do with these changes.

Debriefing while still in-country decreases the outside distractions, and the difficulty of getting everyone back together after you return home. We do try to have a "photo-sharing" party about two weeks after the trip, but this is more social than serious. Usually two to three team members take photos for all to share and digital cameras make it easy to create a CD for each person.

## Questions for Post-Trip Debrief

- What would have helped you to better prepare for the trip?
- How did the trip meet/not meet your expectations?
- Describe one thing that was not what you expected.
- What is your favorite memory from the trip?
- What would you tell someone considering going on a team?
- Describe how your experience on the team changed your viewpoint about missions.
- What experience will you share with someone who asks about your trip?
- How did your experiences change your faith?

## After-Glow

Short-term Missions do change the lives of team members and often, of the church that sent them. The year after our first STM, our church sent the youth group on its first Short-Term Mission project, a second team back to Ecuador and a team to Appalachia to work on a project within the U.S. In addition, we saw a growth in interest in local mission projects at a soup kitchen, Habitat for Humanity, and with an organization serving migrant farmers. The church that initially sent thirteen people into the world was soon sponsoring projects involving more than one hundred people.

Our own teams spread out from our church to other churches and communities. Today, it is common for our teams to include people from twelve or more different churches and places.

What of the impact in the host communities? We have been blessed to be able to return to the same neighborhood for four years. When we first visited Cayambe, the two-year-old church there had thirty-five members. Two years later, it had grown to about 125. We set up a temporary medical clinic in the community center and see almost five hundred people in four days. Obviously, most of them are not members of the church. We treat all and give them the same message: "God bless you," and we are "sharing God's love in practical ways" with them. Both phrases are written in Spanish on stickers on every medication bottle, toothbrush and toothpaste.

The church had grown in four years to the point where they needed a new sanctuary and began to build it. They planned to turn the old one into a clinic and hire a doctor. So, we knew it was time for us to move on to another community.

* * *

John Chapman lived and traveled throughout Ohio and Indiana during the 19th century. I used to think of him scattering seeds as he strolled through the forests. However, in reality, he was an educated and experienced nurseryman. He planted trees and built fences around them to protect them from animals. He would stay long enough to see the nursery become a profitable business, then leave a neighbor in charge and move to another area to begin a new venture. In a year or two, he might return to collect any profits from each of his nurseries, and most of the time, he'd accept cornmeal or used clothing in barter.

What does the story of Johnny Appleseed have to do with Short-Term Missions?

Chapman trained for the job, and he had a plan for orderly planting and protection of his trees. When the time came to leave, he left the nursery in the care of someone he trusted. He did not expect to see profits, but when he did, they met his needs at that moment.

You trained your team for their Short-Term Mission. Together, you planted and nurtured seeds in hearts already prepared by God to receive His message. You left before the harvest, and you might never see the results of your labors, but your profits are measured in the experiences and growth of your team members.

## Returning

What about next year? Should you return to the same site or seek a new mission project? We have done both. There are advantages to going back to one place where you have begun making friends and can continue. You feel more comfortable after several visits and the people may open up more in subsequent visits. You can follow their progress and changes over time.

The greatest danger, however, is creating a dependent relationship in which they expect you to come every year to help them or bring them something. When we began visiting Cayambe, we brought a construction team to work on a four-story building. We helped with the third floor and painted the already finished first floor.

The next year we brought a medical team to the same place and continued that for two more years. We made good friends, and even became godparents to a little boy there.

After the third medical team, we decided we needed to move on, a difficult and emotional decision. The people had begun building a new sanctuary and had plans to convert the former one into a medical clinic and hire part-time medical staff. We knew we had to encourage this positive growth in their community by not bringing back another medical team.

We still keep in touch by occasional email with one of the college-aged girls, and letters from a child we support there at a Compassion International project.

What they ask from us now is prayer because they know we understand their needs and consider them our brothers and sisters.

\* \* \*

*While a large crowd was gathering and people were coming to Jesus from town after town, he told this parable: "A farmer went out to sow his seed. As he was scattering the seed, some fell along the path; it was trampled on, and the birds of the air ate it up. Some fell on rock, and when it came up, the plants withered because they had no moisture.*

*Other seed fell among thorns, which grew up with it and choked the plants. Still other seed fell on good soil. It came up and yielded a crop, a hundred times more than was sown."*
Luke 8: 4-8

## Action Plan

### Personal response:
How will you share your personal story of your short-term mission experience?

### Awareness:
How will you debrief the team?

### Making a Difference:
How will you measure the impact of the STM on your life, your church, and your team?

# Chapter 18

## Visiting Bible School

### Introduction

On our first Short-Term Mission, the team worked on a construction project in the mornings and, in the afternoons, the women left the project to conduct Visiting Bible School (VBS) at a local church. We planned for two-to-three hours with the children, similar to what we experienced at our home church VBS. There would be modules for story time with felt boards and sock puppets, crafts to reinforce the lessons, games and a snack.

When we arrived the first day, we discovered our hosts had in mind a program of only ninety minutes, and the children could not be divided into age-specific groups. We had toddlers to thirteen-year-olds all together on the flat rooftop of the church. We taught them two songs, then had just enough time to rush through the story and start the craft.

The crafts turned out to be more complicated than we anticipated, and most of our "teachers" forgot how to assemble the pipe cleaner animals they'd easily created a few months before. Soon, the children were showing us how to make angels which didn't fit into the Noah's Ark story as well as animals.

194

Our interpreter had stayed with the construction project and only one person on the team could speak Spanish. She quickly became overwhelmed translating stories, songs and craft instructions.

\* \* \*

The next year, we planned much simpler crafts and stories for a four-day VBS. However, the children were on a school holiday and didn't come to the church for VBS. So, we took our lessons and crafts to a neighboring town, going to a public school where the administration happily allowed us to visit for two hours.

Because of our preparations and three months of rehearsals, we were able to move into the impromptu setting quickly and efficiently. Every adult understood the crafts and helped the children, even though none of us could speak Spanish. We were surprised when the craft glue didn't set up in forty-degree weather—or perhaps the problem was the 11,000 foot elevation. Fortunately, we also had glue sticks with us.

We had taped the dialogue of a puppet show in Spanish and planned to act it out with the puppets. However, the tape recorder batteries died and I had not brought extras. Our translator stepped in and read the script while the puppets nodded and pretended to speak.

\* \* \*

Visiting Bible School is never an after-thought, or an "extra" tacked on to fill down time after the "real" project. Teaching children is the **most important** task you will ever have on a Short-Term Mission. Through them, you also reach the family and the community. The stories you share, the crafts they make, and the songs they learn will stay with them for a lifetime. You may never know the impact your efforts have.

## Flexibility

Planning and preparation are essential elements for VBS, but the key to success is flexibility. When you plan for a dozen kids, two hundred may show up. When you purchase 100 foam craft kits, the students will be on school holiday. The groups of children are often mixed ages because older children have responsibility for younger siblings.

## Hints for Handling a Crowd

- Enlist the help of teachers and mothers. Explaining a craft project or story in advance enables them to translate for you, or to assist the children with the project.
- Let the teachers and mothers keep order. You are a guest in their home.
- Schedule music as the first activity to allow time for children to come in and find a seat.
- Music will also attract more children.
- If there are no children at a church site, ask to visit a school. In some countries, schools allow groups to come in. Try to make arrangements with the school officials in advance.
- Save games and snacks for the last activities of the day, giving the kids something to look forward to.

Craft projects often present challenges to adults who vaguely remember their kindergarten days. Directions get separated from the project. Batteries die and scissors disappear.

## Tips for Painless Craft Projects

- Buy canvas tool belts (about one dollar each at a building supply store) for each adult. The pockets can hold scissors, a roll of tape, a bottle of glue, a small ruler, pencil sharpener, stickers, marking pens, pencils, etc. They roll up and pack easily with the supplies in the pockets.

196

- Have crafts for two or three different-aged groups in the same room. Younger ones can color a page while older ones create a more elaborate craft.
- The cheapest white paper plates are great for coloring projects. You can glue a picture to them, punch a hole and thread a piece of yarn through it so the project can be hung or worn. Cut in half and colored, plates become rainbows.
- Poster putty can be used to hang pictures and posters on almost any surface, even concrete. It is easily removed and reusable. Caution: it may leave an oily residue on some painted walls, so check in an inconspicuous place first.
- Do any cutting in advance. Many children have difficulty using scissors if they are not accustomed to them, and if you have a large group, cutting can be time-consuming.
- Try to provide one adult for every half-dozen children.
- When a craft has several parts to be assembled, pack them in zippered-closure bags. One craft per bag is best, but if you don't have that many bags, put several together.
- Dump crayons out of their boxes and pack in a plastic bag. You can give each child two-or three and let them trade for other colors.
- Pack colored or regular pencils and scissors the same way.
- Glue sticks and glue dots are much easier to use than glue.

If you can afford them, craft kits are an easy way to provide all the supplies for a project. The drawback, however, is: you must have the exact number of kits and you may not know how many to bring. Additional supplies may be unavailable and the local teacher will not be able to replicate the project at a later time.

## About Craft Kits

- The Oriental Trading Company catalogue offers pre-cut foam crafts at reasonable prices.
- Assemble at least one kit in advance to serve as a model.
- Pre-glue some items if you don't have sufficient time for the entire project.
- Projects often need to be left overnight to dry.
- Craft glue may not work under some environmental conditions.
- Blank pages of a children's drawing tablet make excellent placemats for glue projects.

Coordinating the message of the story or lesson and the craft is easy if you have a brief "theme." We write the theme on neon-colored stickers and give each child one when they arrive. For example, ""El Dios nos ama," ("God loves us,") or "Jesus es el pan de vida," ("Jesus is the bread of life.")

## Stickers

- Kids love stickers with pictures on them. Animal stickers illustrate the story of Creation or Noah's Ark and can be used in a game in which they must find another child with the same sticker.
- Plain white or colorful label stickers can be used for name tags.
- Stickers are wonderful rewards for memorizing verses.

## Changing Lives

In spite of all the challenges, great things happen when you tell children the story of God's love for them. A little boy, attending his first VBS at a church, learned a song about Jesus. He told his mother about the music, lessons and crafts, and insisted she must come the next day. She'd never been to a church before, but agreed to visit.

When she came, a team member greeted her with a song booklet and invited her to join as we sang with the children. Then, she met a missionary and the pastor of the church and spent more than an hour in a conversation which changed her life, and that of her whole family.

* * *

VBS can also change your team members' lives. Linda, a retired nurse, decided after working in a medical clinic that on her next trip, she would prefer to work in VBS. She was very anxious during the preparations because she had never undertaken the responsibility for five days of VBS, and because the team was small, she'd be on her own. With the help of the team leader, she put together a lesson plan, collected craft supplies.

The first day of VBS, two teenaged girls offered to help. Linda took advantage of their help and spent four days talking with them about Christ and their lives. She encouraged them to stay in school and try to continue their education beyond high school. They made special gifts to give her on the last day.

The next year, Linda had greater confidence in her ability to manage VBS and needed less help from the leader to create plans and collect supplies. The two girls she had befriended the year before showed up and they renewed their friendships.

* * *

## Music

- Create a CD or cassette tape of praise songs and children's songs, preferably in the language of the country, for team members to learn in the weeks before the STM.
- Print extra song sheets for your hosts or make posters with the words.

- Kazoos, clackers, maracas and finger cymbals are fun ways to enhance the music.
- Bring along a small CD or cassette player with speakers, or use an MP3 or I-Pod.
- Remember an extra set of batteries for the player and speakers.

## Fun and Games

Bottles of blow bubbles are the most popular item to bring to VBS. Give the bottles to adults and let the children chase the bubbles. Silly String™ is also a hit with older children, but caution them not to eat it. We also like "glow-in-the-dark" bracelets and use them to talk about Jesus being the "light of the world."

## Fun Activities

- Balloon animals are easy to make; instructions come with a small hand pump. But you need a head start to create enough of them since everyone wants one as soon as you start making them.

- Sidewalk chart for impromptu artwork and setting up games such as Hop Skotch and 4-Square.

- An inflatable globe ball is a wonderful way to show children where you live and where they live and talk about creation and God's love for all people.

- Soccer balls, footballs, basketballs, and kick balls can all be deflated for packing and re-inflated with a small hand pump.

- A colorful parachute lends itself to many different types of play, and gives everyone a good work out.

## Culturally-Sensitive VBS

You face unique situations as you plan VBS within another culture and language. Behavior has never been a problem for us, even when we have had only four team members working with 200 kids. The children who attend our VBS programs are usually eager to learn and participate. They sing with great enthusiasm, and, like children anywhere, they love to take home a craft project.

Sensitivity to the culture and environment when you choose projects and supplies, means, for example, avoiding making macaroni necklaces in a country where people do not have enough food. The temperature and altitude can impact your plans, as we found out when trying to use white glue. We also try to consider what waste we might generate in countries where trash collection is a problem. In some cultures, certain colors have specific meaning. In Asia, white is the color of mourning; decorating white t-shirts might not be acceptable.

Stories and lessons can be just as challenging as finding appropriate crafts. One year, we used butterflies as the theme for VBS. We had several butterfly crafts, stickers, artwork, etc. We had a puppet show about a caterpillar creating its cocoon, hatching to become a butterfly, to demonstrate how the love of God changes us. After we left, however, we wondered if the children, who had never heard of Jesus, now thought He was a butterfly.

* * *

*"He called a little child and had him stand among them. And he said: 'I tell you the truth, unless you change and become like little children, you will never enter the kingdom of heaven. Therefore, whoever humbles himself like this child is the greatest in the kingdom of heaven.'"*
Matthew 18: 2-4

## Action Plan

### Personal response:
Ask your host if there is an opportunity for VBS.
Begin preparations for lessons, crafts and games.

### Awareness:
Involve the whole team in VBS if possible.

### Making a Difference:
The project is not important; the craft, game and music are not the goal; changing the lives of children is always the priority.

# Chapter 19

## Visiting Bible School II: Lesson Plans

### Stories, Activities and Crafts

The lesson plans in this chapter can be mixed and matched as you wish. Appropriate age levels are indicated by "Beginner," ages 3-6 and "Intermediate," ages 7 and older. Try to coordinate stories, activities and crafts around a theme, and use questions or drama to engage the children's interest. Print the theme, in the children's language, on colorful stickers to give to them each day. You can also find music to support the theme or stories.

### Suggest Lesson Plans:

| Theme | Story | Activity | Craft |
|---|---|---|---|
| God loves you | God Made the World<br>The Tower | The Snake in the Garden<br>Animal Charades | Fingerprint Bugs<br>Fox and Hens |
| God provides | Rain, Rain<br>Noah's Ark<br>Joseph's Coat<br>Ruth | Animal Follow the Leader<br>Duck, Duck, Goose<br>Animal Concentration | Rainbow Mobile<br>Joseph & the Coat |
| God has a plan | Father Abraham<br>Baby Moses<br>The Giant | Abraham & Isaac | Baby in a Basket |

| Theme | Story | Activity | Craft |
|---|---|---|---|
| Jesus is God's Son | When Jesus was a Baby<br>Three Wise Men | 3 Trees<br>The Birth of Jesus | Handprint Chain<br>Christmas Card<br>Mobile |
| God sent Jesus | The Fishes & Loaves<br><br>Jesus Calms the Storm | Fishers of Men<br>String Game | Fish Paper Plate |
| God changes us | Caterpillar to Butterfly<br>The Blind Man<br>Steve & Phil's Excellent Adventure | Butterfly Drama<br>Light of the World<br>Blind Man's Bluff | Butterfly Crafts<br>Butterfly Bookmarks<br>Caterpillar & Cocoon |
| God saves us | The Good Samaritan<br>Zaccheus<br>A Surprise!<br>The Spirit, the Wind & the Fire | A Boy Named Cornelius | Freeze Tag<br>Chains of Love |

# Stories:

## God Made the World (Beginners)

Look up.  What do you see?  The sky?  Clouds?  The sun?  Or perhaps, stars?  Birds?  A butterfly?

God made all of them.
Look around you. What do you see?  A tree?  Flowers?  Grass?  Or maybe, A river?  A hill?  A mountain?

God made all of them.
Listen.  What do you hear?  A dog barking?  A rooster crowing?  A bee buzzing?

God made all of them.
Take a deep breath. God made the air you breathe, the water you drink, the food you eat.

Look down. Wiggle your toes.  Stomp your feet.  Jump high in the air.
Stretch out your arms. Wave your hands.  Clap them together. Touch your fingers to your nose.  Wriggle your nose.  Make a big smile.  Wrap your arms around yourself in a big hug.

God made you, too.

* * *

## God Made the World (Intermediate)

In the beginning, God made the heavens and the earth.  There was nothing but darkness all around and wind swept over the water.  Then God said, "Let there be light!"  God saw that the light was good.  God divided the light from the darkness. The light was called Day and the dark was called Night.  This was the first day.

On the second day, God made the sky.  On the third day, God said, "Let the waters gather together and let the dry land appear."  The land became the earth; the water became the seas.  Next God made wonderful things grow from the earth—all sorts of beautiful plants. God saw that this was good.

Then, on the fourth day, God made two great lights, the sun for the day and the moon for night.  God made millions and millions of stars, placing them in the heavens to shine. Again God saw how good it was,

On the fifth day, God looked to the water, creating every living thing in the sea, from the smallest creature to the greatest sea monsters.  Next, God looked to the sky, creating all the flying birds. God blessed the creatures, telling them, "Go forth; fill up the waters and the sky."  God saw that this was good.

On the sixth day, God said, "Let the earth be filled with living creatures: cattle, creeping things and wild animals of every kind."  And it was so.  God saw that it was good.  God looked around at all the beautiful things and all the wonderful creatures on the land, in the water, and in the sky. Then, God said, "Let us make people! They will be in charge of the fish, the birds, the cattle, the wild animals and the creeping, crawling creatures of the earth. They will be special to me."

God created man and woman. They were made in the image of God. God blessed them, saying, "Fill up the earth. Rule over it. I have given you plants, trees, birds, animals and all living creatures.

Now, on the seventh day, God was finished with the work of creation and rested. God blessed the seventh day and made it holy.

Questions:
1. Why did God make people?
2. How do we thank God for creating the world and everything in it?
3. How do we care for animals and the earth?

* * *

## The Tower

Did you know that a long time ago, everyone spoke the same language. There was no Spanish, English, French or Chinese. Everyone could understand everyone else.

The people decided to build a tall tower. So tall that it would reach heaven.

"This tower will make us famous," they said proudly. "We can reach God."

They started building. Brick after brick. But their pride made God angry. He changed the words they spoke so that they each spoke a different language.

A man would ask another one for a brick and instead, he'd get a hammer. Can you imagine? Or he'd ask for a shovel and get a glass of water. How confusing! They couldn't build the tower that way!

Today, we speak many different languages today, but we all share God's love. Our words for God and love may be different, but we are all His children. We have found new ways to share God's love. How? With a handshake, or a smile, or a hug. How can you tell someone about God?

* * *

## Rain, Rain

Can you remember a time when it rained day after day? Maybe you thought it would never stop. What if it rained for forty days? A long time ago, God sent rain for forty days and forty nights. A great flood covered the whole earth. But one man and his family were safe. The man's name was Noah.

Noah was a good man who loved God. God saved Noah because he obeyed God. God told Noah to build a boat big enough for his whole family and for animals. When Noah began to build the boat, people called him crazy.

"We live in a desert," they said. "There are no oceans here."

"Why are you building a big boat?" They laughed at him, but he kept building his boat.

When it was finished, he put food in it. And God told him to gather two of every animal. Then, the rains started. It rained and rained and rained. The water covered all the land, but Noah and his family and the animals were safe and dry in their big boat. When the rain finally stopped, Noah sent a bird to see if there was any dry land anywhere. The bird didn't find any. He waited a week and tried again. This time the bird returned with an olive branch—he had found dry land.

God gave Noah a promise that he would never again send a flood to cover the whole earth. As a sign of that promise, he put a rainbow in the sky. Whenever you see a rainbow, you can remember that God had a plan and a promise.

\* \* \*

## Noah's Ark

God was angry—angry enough to punish the world because so many people had done evil things. But God did see one man who was kind and good and obeyed the law. The man's name was Noah. Noah and his family loved God.

God decided to send a great flood to destroy the earth. First, God spoke to Noah. God said, "Make a boat of wood. You and your family will go into the boat and be safe inside when I send a flood to the world."

God told Noah exactly how to build the boat and Noah did as God told him. God told him to store food in the boat also. He put rooms in the boat for people and animals. Yes, animals! God told Noah, "Take the animals into the boat, two of every kind."

Noah did what God said.

He finished the boat and waited for God's command. When the time came, God told Noah and his family to climb into the boat and bring in the animals two-by-two. When they were all in the boat and the door was closed, the rain began. It rained hard for forty days and forty nights. Soon water covered everything. But Noah and his family and the animals were safe inside the boat.

Finally, it stopped raining. Noah sent a bird out into the sky. It could not find any place to land. So he waited. After seven days, Noah sent out a dove. This time the bird returned with an olive branch in its beak. The land was beginning to dry out and

the birds could live in the trees.
Then, God said to Noah, "Go out of the boat; you are safe."

Noah and his family and all of the animals came out of the boat. And God placed a rainbow in the sky as his promise that he would never again destroy the earth with a flood.

Questions:
1. Why was it important that Noah obey God?
2. What was the special sign God gave Noah to show his promise to never again destroy the world with a flood?

* * *

## Joseph's Coat (Intermediate)

Joseph was the youngest and favorite son of a man named Jacob. Jacob loved the boy so much that he made him a special coat of many colors. This made his other brothers very angry and jealous. One day, when the brothers were tending their sheep, Jacob sent Joseph out with a message for them.

The brothers were so angry with Joseph that some of them wanted to kill him. Instead, they threw him into a pit and left him while they tried to decide what to do with him. While they were eating dinner and talking about their plans, a group of traders came along. The brothers sold Joseph to the traders and then took the coat of many colors and put blood on it so that their father would believe their story that Joseph had been killed by a wild animal.

The traders took Joseph to Egypt where he became a slave in the household of one of the king's guards. After many difficulties, Joseph ended up as an advisor to the king of Egypt. The king had a dream and asked Joseph what it meant. Joseph told him there would be seven years of good crops followed by seven years of no rain and bad crops. The king filled his warehouses with food for the seven bad years, and his people did not starve.

Jacob and his other sons were starving. They came to Egypt to ask for food. The man in charge was Joseph and when they realized it was their brother, they were afraid he'd try to get even with them. But he didn't; he opened his arms to welcome them. God had saved him many times and now he saved his family and shared God's love with them.

Questions:
1. What special plan did God have for Joseph?

* * *

## Ruth (Intermediate)

In a faraway land, there lived a woman named Ruth.

She had been married to the son of Naomi, but her husband and Naomi's husband had both died. And now, Naomi wanted to go back to the land of her family. When she got ready to leave, Ruth said, "Wherever you go, I will go. I will stay with you. Your people will be my people and your God will be my God."
Even though Ruth didn't know Naomi's family or Naomi's God, she trusted Naomi.

They traveled until they reached the land of Naomi's family. When they got there, Ruth went to work on a farm picking up grain after the harvest so that they would have food to eat.

The farm belonged to a man named Boaz. He knew that Ruth was helping Naomi and he began to fall in love with her. Ruth knew Boaz was a good man and she married him.

God can change lives when we trust Him.

Questions:
1. How can God change someone's life?
2. What does it mean to trust in God?

\* \* \*

## Abraham, Our Father (Intermediate)

Abraham was a man who lived in a place called Ur. He believed in the one, true God when most other people worshipped many gods. When he was an old man, God told him to leave his family home and move to a different place. God wanted to get him away from those who worshipped other gods. Abraham had faith in God and he and his wife left their home to travel west and north to the land of Canaan.

Next, God promised He would make Abraham the "Father of Nations." This meant that his children and grand-children and descendants would be more than all the stars in the sky.

But Abraham, who was one hundred years old, didn't have any children with his wife Sarah. They wondered exactly how God would fulfill his promise when she was too old to have a child.

In fact, Sarah laughed when Abraham told her that she would have a baby.

And God said to Abraham, "Why did Sarah laugh? Is there anything that is too hard for God to do?"

One year later, they had a baby boy and they named him Isaac.

\* \* \*

## Baby Moses (Beginner)

How great surprise! There is a baby in a basket!
The baby is called Moses. His mother put him in the basket to hide him from a bad king. The basket floats and floats down the river.
A princess finds Moses in the basket. She picks him up and looks around for his mother. The princess takes Moses to her

house. God protected the baby from the bad king.
Questions:
1. Who is in the basket?
2. Who put him in the basket?
3. Who found Moses?

* * *

## Baby Moses (Intermediate)

In the land named Egypt, there was a king called Pharaoh. The Pharaoh ruled his own people and had slaves from the country of Israel. There were so many people from Israel that the Pharaoh became afraid that they might try to take over his country. So, Pharaoh decided to get rid of all the baby boys from the slave families.

One mother had baby boy and wanted to hide him from the king. She got a basket big enough to hold him, then put the baby into the basket. She carried the basket to a river and put it in the water. The baby's sister Miriam hid along the shore and watched the baby to be sure he was safe. She saw the Pharaoh's daughter, the princess, came down to the river to bathe. The princess wanted to know what was inside the basket. She found the baby boy and decided to keep him.

The princess named the baby, "Moses," which means "I drew him out of the water." The princess adopted the baby boy and he grew up in the king's palace. Moses would grow up to lead his people out of their slavery in Egypt.

Questions:
1. Many people have names with special meanings.
2. Do you know what your name means?
3. God had a plan to save Moses' life when he was a small baby. What plan do you think God has for your life?

## The Giant

There was a giant who was an enemy of the God's people, the Israelites. He led an army against the Israelites and no one wanted to fight him because he was so big and mean. A young shepherd boy named David had brothers serving in the army. His father called him from the fields one day and asked him to take some bread to his brothers. When David got there, he heard about Goliath, the giant.

"I will fight him," he said.

Everyone laughed at this little boy who would fight a giant.

"God will help me," David said.

The soldiers gave him a sword and helmet but they were so heavy he couldn't even lift them. Instead, he went to a stream and picked up five small, smooth rocks. The giant came close, but David was not afraid. He trusted God. He put a stone in his slingshot and threw it at Goliath. The stone hit the giant right on his forehead. Goliath fell down and the war was over.

God can use anyone, even a young child, if we trust in him.

\* \* \*

## When Jesus was a Baby

Jesus was once a baby just like you were. He had ten toes, and ten fingers, and hair, just like yours. He had a mama who loved him very much. Before he was born, an angel visited his mother Mary and told her she would have a baby, and she would name him "Jesus." Mary was very surprised, but the angel told her this was all part of God's plan.

So, Mary and her husband Joseph waited for the birth of the baby. While they waited, they heard that they would have to go to another town, Bethlehem. When they arrived there, many other people were there also so there was no place for them to stay.

They found a soft bed of hay in a stable. And Mary gave birth to her baby there. She wrapped him in cloth and laid him in a manger, which was the feeding box for the animals that lived in the stable.

That night, angels appeared to shepherds in the hills near Bethlehem. The angels told the shepherds the good news that a baby had been born, and they would find him lying in a manger. The shepherds hurried to the stable and knelt down to see the baby Jesus. We still celebrate the birth of the baby Jesus now many, many years later.

* * *

## Three Wise Men

A star appeared in the sky. An unusual star, very large and very bright. The kind of star that might appear when a king is born. Three men from the East studied the stars and were especially interested in that star.

"We must follow the star and see where it points," they decided.

So, they prepared for a trip and they brought gifts with them for the baby, the son of a king. When they arrived in the land where the star brought them, they found the baby Jesus. They gave him gifts, frankincense, myrrh and gold.

What strange gifts to give a baby! But gifts that honored Jesus as the son of God, the Son of Man and the King of Kings.

What gift would you give to the baby Jesus?

* * *

## The Fishes and the Loaves

One day, Jesus came to a place where many, many people had gathered to hear him speak.  He talked all day and when night came, he began to feel sorry for them because many of them did not bring food with them.
His friends asked him to send the people home, but instead he said, "Give them
something to eat."

They looked at each other and said, "Where can we find food for everyone.  There is only a boy here and he has five loaves of bread and two fishes."  They knew that would never be enough to feed so many people.

Jesus told them to bring the fishes and loaves to him.  He held the fishes and loaves and blessed them.  Then he gave them to his friends to pass out among the crowd.  Everyone ate until they were full. When the men collected what was left over, they filled twelve baskets!

* * *

## Jesus Calms the Storm (Intermediate)

Jesus had been teaching people near a lake when he became tired.  He told his friends he wanted to go to the other side of the lake.  They got into their boat and began to sail across the lake while Jesus fell asleep in the back of the boat.

A great storm came up, with blowing wind and waves that crashed into the boat, nearly filling it with water.  Some of the men thought the boat might sink and they would drown.  They woke up Jesus with their cries, "Teacher!  Do you not care that we are sinking!"

Jesus asked, "Why are you afraid?"

216

Then, he said to the wind and the waves, "Peace, be still!" The wind stopped blowing and the waves calmed down. The storm passed and the lake was once again calm and quiet.

Jesus' friends were amazed and looked at each other saying, "Even the wind and the waves obey Jesus."

Questions:
1. Have you ever been afraid and wanted to ask Jesus for help?
2. How can you call on Jesus?

* * *

## Caterpillar to Butterfly

A beautiful butterfly wasn't always so pretty. Butterflies begin as caterpillars, crawling along the ground. The caterpillar crawls up onto the stem or leaf of a plant and slowly weaves itself into a cocoon. Then it sleeps and waits. After a time, the cocoon breaks open and out flies a beautiful butterfly.

Like the caterpillar, we aren't always so pretty. We have sin in our hearts. Then Jesus comes into our lives and our hearts, and we break out of a cocoon of sin. Because of Jesus, we are beautiful in God's eyes.

* * *

## The Blind Man

There was a man who could not see. Not flowers. Not birds. Not the sun in the sky. He was blind all of his life. He couldn't find his way around and needed help from his friends. Jesus saw him and felt sorry for him.

Without saying a word to the man, Jesus bent down and picked up some dirt and spit on it and put it on the man's eyes. Then, he told the man to go and wash the mud off his eyes. When the man did that, he could see!

Jesus had healed him.

Sometimes we are blind, too. We can't see what God wants us to see. We need for Jesus to heal us, too

\* \* \*

## Steve & Phil's Excellent Adventure  (Intermediate)

Steve and Phil were friends. They were waiters in a restaurant and they told people about Jesus. Sometimes, they performed miracles, but they always told people, "God is responsible for all we do."

Many people didn't understand them and complained to the police who arrested Steve and Phil. At their trial, the witnesses lied. But when the judges looked at Steve, they saw an angels' faces. They became scared and asked for an explanation.

Steve, not the least bit afraid, spoke right up and told them about the many times God had used special people such s Abraham, Moses and David to save his people from their evil ways. Then Jesus came. And now, the people had killed Jesus, the son of God. This was more than the crowd could bear to hear, and they dragged Steve out of town. They threw stones at him until they killed him.

Phil, in the meanwhile, lost his job and went to a city in a nearby country. It turned out to be a place where he could share God with everyone he met, and not have to be afraid they'd arrest him. Phil did good things, too, healing sick people, preaching the Word of God, baptizing and performing miracles so that everyone would know that Jesus was the son of God. He even went to Africa to tell people about Jesus and many people listened to him.

God used these two men, whose jobs were small and unimportant, to do great things. Both men had a message to share and both gave their lives to God.

Questions:

    1. Can God use an ordinary person like Steve and Phil to do great things?

    2. What would you do if God asked you to go someplace you've never been before?

    3. Would you tell others about God even if you didn't know them?

* * *

## The Good Samaritan (Intermediate)

Once a man asked Jesus, "Who is my neighbor?"

Jesus answered with this story. "A man was traveling on a road when robbers grabbed him. They took all his clothes and beat him, then left him half-dead and bleeding. Soon a holy man came down the road. He saw the man but he did not stop. He passed him by. Then another man came along and he, too, passed by the injured man.

Finally, a Samaritan, a man who was from a different land, and therefore, not liked came by. He felt sorry for the hurt man. He helped the man by cleaning his wounds and giving him new clothing. Then, he picked him up and carried him to a place where he could stay until he was healthy."

When Jesus was done telling the story, he asked "Which of the three men was a neighbor to the man who was robbed and hurt?"

The man answered, "The one who was kind to him."

Jesus said, "You should be like the Samaritan. Treat all people with kindness. We are all neighbors to one another."

Questions:
1. Who is your neighbor?
2. Why would someone who wasn't liked be kind to a stranger?
3. How can you help others?

\* \* \*

## Zaccheus

I'm going to tell you a story about a man named Zaccheus. Every time I say his name, I want you to say, "Booo!" (Practice a few times. The "boos" should sound menacing. Then as the story is told, be sure to allow time for the booing.)

No one liked Zaccheus. (Boo!) He was a tax collector and a wealthy man. Tax collectors were disliked because they sometimes cheated people by collecting more than they should. They gave part of the money to the government and kept the rest for themselves.

Zaccheus (Boo!) wasn't liked. And he didn't even like himself. He was short. Very short. So short that he could not see over the heads of other people when he was with them.

One day Zaccheus (boo!) heard that a man named Jesus was coming to town. Everyone was excited to see and hear Jesus because they knew he was a teacher who did many good things. Zaccheus (boo!) wanted to see Jesus and hear his words just like everyone else. But Zaccheus (Boo!) was too short and would never be able to see Jesus unless…unless…unless…he climbed up in a tree.

Zaccheus (boo!) did just that! He climbed up in a tree so that he could see Jesus when he walked past. But Jesus didn't walk past! He stopped. Right under the tree and he looked up. When he saw Zaccheus (boo!), a strange thing happened.

Jesus smiled at the short man and said, "Zaccheus, come down from there. I want to go to your house for dinner."

To go to Zaccheus' house for dinner mean that he was a friend of Jesus. Even someone whom everyone hated. Even someone who cheated people and stole their money. Even someone who didn't like himself because he was short. Jesus is a friend to all people.

Zaccheus was sorry for the bad things he had done. He told Jesus that he would give half of his money to the poor, and if he had cheated anybody out of anything, he would give back four times that amount. Jesus was pleased with this. Zaccheus had a change in his heart because he met Jesus.

Questions:
1. Why did people dislike Zaccheus?
2. What did Zaccheus think about himself?
3. What did Zaccheus do to see Jesus?
4. What did Jesus do?
5. How can we be friends with Jesus?

\* \* \*

## A Surprise!

When Jesus died, his body was taken to a cave that would be his tomb. A huge stone was rolled across the doorway. Then, two soldiers guarded the door to be sure no one went in. No one could go in, but they didn't count on someone coming out!

On Sunday morning, there was an earthquake, and an angel came from heaven to roll the stone away. The guards were so afraid that they fell down in a faint.

One of Jesus' friends, a woman named Mary came to the tomb that morning. She saw the stone had been moved. When she looked inside the tomb, the angel said to her, "Jesus is not here.  He is alive.  Go tell his friends."

Mary ran to tell the others.  Jesus was alive!  They didn't have to be sad or afraid.  Jesus was alive!  And he really was!

Because Jesus rose from the dead, we know that we, too, can have eternal life with him.

* * *

## The Spirit, the Wind & the Fire (Intermediate)

The disciples met in a room as they had done almost every day since Jesus left them.  They were waiting...they weren't sure what for...perhaps Jesus would return.  He promised to send someone to them.  They didn't know when, or who, or where.  So they stayed together and waited.

Just before dawn, as the sky was turning purple, then pink, then orange, and the early birds stretched, flapped their wings and crowed, the men began to wake up.  The room was filled with excitement, but no one knew why.

Suddenly, wind began to blow as if every window were open, but it came from nowhere and blew in every direction at once.  At first, little puffs of air grew into a steady breeze, then into gusts, then a blast of wind roared and blew from wall to wall, corner to corner.  Suddenly it stopped as quickly as it had started.  The disciples were startled, amazed and afraid.

Little tongues of fire appeared, floating in the air above each person's head.  And, the Holy Spirit filled each person. They began to speak and pray in languages they did not know or understand. One by one the men came out of the house and spoke to the crowd.  Their strange behavior attracted a large crowd outside the house.

Many people from foreign lands were visiting in the city because of a holiday.  When the disciples spoke, each person understood what they were saying even though they spoke many different languages. The disciples told the crowd about Jesus and many people believed.

Questions:
1. Has God ever done something exciting in your life?

\* \* \*

## Dramas, Puppet Skits

### The Snake in the Garden

*Characters: Narrator, Snake, Eve*

**Narrator:** When God made man and woman, He gave them a special place to live, called the Garden of Eden. He told them they could eat the fruit of any tree in the garden, except one. They should not eat the fruit of the tree of the Knowledge of Good and Bad. In that tree, there lived a snake. And one day, as the woman, Eve, was walking in the garden, she met the snake.

**Snake:** I just love this garden. I can slide and slip and slink and slither all around the branches of this wonderful tree. And when I get tired, I just wrap myself around a limb and soak up the sun. Oh, the snake's life is for me. But sometimes, I get bored. I think, there's got to be more to life than this tree, even if it is in Eden. This place is so perfect it's boring. So, I'm thinking we need a little action around here. Hey, here comes someone. It's the woman. Woo-hoo, oh, Woman!

**Eve:** Who's that calling me?

**Snake:** Up here! Look up! Yo! I'm in the tree.

**Eve:** Oh! Who are you and what are you doing in that tree?

**Snake:** I'm your friendly snake. Just hanging around this tree.

**Eve**: Wait a minute...I remember this tree. It's the one God called the "tree of the Knowledge of Good and Bad." He said we could eat the fruit of any other tree in the garden but not this one.

**Snake**: What does he know? This fruit is the best in the whole place. I bet He was just saying that because He wanted it all for Himself.

**Eve**: He said that we should not even touch it, for if we did, we'd surely die.

**Snake**: Naaawwww! You will not die. Not only that, but if you eat it, your eyes will be opened and you will be like God. Look at this fruit. It's is wonderful. The tastiest in the whole garden. You want it, don't you? Just one small bite. A nibble. No one will ever know.

**Eve**: It does look good. And tastes even better. I should show my husband. He'll want to try it as well.

**Narrator**: So, the woman ate, and offered the fruit to her husband, and he ate, too. When God learned that they had eaten the forbidden fruit, He made them leave the garden. And evil came into the world that had been perfect.

\* \* \*

### Abraham and Isaac

*Characters: Abraham, Angel, Isaac*

**Abraham**: Isaac, son, let's take a walk.

**Isaac**: Where are we going, father?

**Abraham**: We're going to climb up that mountain. Help me carry this wood. We're going to make a sacrifice to God today as he asked me to do.

**Isaac**: You seem sad, father. Is everything all right?

**Abraham**: There are times when God asks us to do something and we may not understand why, but we must do it anyway because of faith and obedience. Do you see that flat rock over there? We'll use that for our sacrifice. Pile the wood on it and use the hot coals I brought to start a fire.

**Isaac**: Father, we have the wood and the fire, but where is the lamb for the offering?

**Abraham**: God himself will provide the lamb for the offering.
*(Isaac wanders off and Abraham prays)*

**Abraham**: I will do as you have commanded, God, but my heart is heavy. I will offer you my son, whom I love because I love you more.

**Angel**: Abraham! Abraham! Do not lay your hand on the boy. Your obedience is well known to me. Look there in the bushes and you will find a ram for your sacrifice.

\* \* \*

### 3 Trees

*Characters: Narrator and 3 characters who are trees*
**Narrator:** This is the story of three trees planted side by side in the forest. They started as small seedlings and grew proud and tall, stretching their limbs out to the skies.
(*Three tree characters stretch their arms up.*)

They tried to outdo each other, each one wanting to be the tallest and best. Each one would say, "See, I am the tallest and the best. My branches reach high into the sky. I hold them up to praise God. Surely, He will bless me greatly."

One afternoon, a man came into the forest and cut down the tallest of the trees.
(*One tree leans and falls down.*)

The tree was cut up in many small pieces which were fitted together for a feed box. The man was very pleased with his feed box and put it in his stable. The box complained, "How can I praise and glorify God now? I am a lowly feed box in a small barn. I hold hay for animals now." How could the box know that a few months later, a baby would be born in that stable and wrapped in rags and laid in the box, for want of a proper bed?
(*Fallen tree exits.*)

The two remaining trees continued to try to be the tallest and best in their praise of God. Years later, men came into the forest again and cut down the second tree.
(*Second tree leans and falls.*)

They cut it into long planks and built a boat. The tree complained, "I was once tall and straight and lifted my branches to praise God. Now I float on the water and smell like fish." Little did the tree know about the man, who was a friend of the fishermen, and who came on the boat one day. He stood on the wide, flat planks to speak about God to a crowd of people sitting on the shore.
(*Second tree exits.*)

Shortly after that, the third tree was cut down and fashioned into a cross.
(*Tree remains standing but holds arms out like a cross.*)

The cross cried, "I was once the tallest tree in the forest and lifted my branches higher than any other to praise God. Now, I am a cross on which a man will hang and die." Above the man's head there hung a sign which said, "Jesus of Nazareth, King of the Jews."

The trees wanted to praise and glorify God, but they didn't understand that in allowing Him to use them in His way, they brought the greatest and best honor to God. God's ways don't always follow our plans and goals, but allowing Him to use us in His way is always the best way to praise and glorify Him.

* * *

## The Birth of Baby Jesus

*Characters: 2 puppets*

**Puppet 1**: The Bible tells us the story of Jesus' birth. I wonder what it was like that night when the baby Jesus was born. The story begins in the little town of Bethlehem where so many people had come to register for a census that the inns were full and no rooms were left. A man named Joseph and his wife Mary who was about to have a baby could find no place to stay.

**Puppet 2**: Finally an inn-keeper felt sorry for them and let them stay in the stable behind his inn.

**Puppet 1**: The inns were crowded and so was the night sky!

**Puppet 2**: Yes, but first let's tell about the shepherds. That's my favorite part.

**Puppet 1**: There were shepherds in the fields, watching their sheep when angels appeared to them.

**Puppet 2**: Yeah, angels. Wow! Can you imagine angels appearing to give you a message from God? Straight from God. They said: "Do not be afraid." An angel telling you not to be afraid! I'd be so surprised I wouldn't know what to say.

**Puppet 1**: That'd be a first. I'd like to see you speechless! Get on with the story.

**Puppet 2**:  OK, so this angel dude, he's standing there talking to the shepherds and he says, "Behold!"  That's another great angel word.  Hardly anyone else ever says "Behold!"

**Puppet 1**:  Ahem!  The story..."

**Puppet 2**:  Yeah, yeah, the angel said, "Behold I bring you good tidings of great joy which shall be for all people.  For there is born to you this day in the city of David, a Savior who is Christ the Lord.  And this shall be a sign to you, you will find the baby wrapped in swaddling clothes, lying in a manger.

**Puppet 1**:  And suddenly, the sky was full of angels saying, "Glory to God in the Highest and on earth peace and goodwill to all men."

**Puppet 2**:  And the shepherds went to the stable and there was the baby just as the angels had said.  And they praised God for all they had seen and heard.

* * *

## Fishers of Men

*Characters: a mother and son*
**John**: (singing) I will make you fishers of men....if you follow me.

**Mom**: John, what's that you're singing?

**John**: "Fishers of Men." Do you want to hear it?

**Mom**: Sure

**John**: I will make you fishers of men....

**Mom**: Do you know what that means, John?

**John**: I didn't till I learned about it at church.

**Mom**: Tell me what you learned.

**John**: Well the pastor said that instead of fishing for fish, God wants us to fish for people.

**Mom**: That's right, John.

**John**: It is not only right, but it works.

**Mom:** What do you mean it works?

**John**: Well, when it was time for church I went over to Joe's house and asked him to go with me.

**Mom**: What did Joe do?

**John**: He asked me a lot of questions like, what do we do, is it fun?

**Mom**: And what did you say?

**John**: I told him that we learn about the Bible and have lots of fun.

**Mom**: And, did he go?

**John**: He sure did and we went to Mark's house and asked him and he came with us, too.

**Mom**: It sounds like you really do know what it means to be fishers of men

**John**: It was fun and I think I had a good fishing trip.

**Mom**: I hope you'll be a fisherman for Jesus as long as you live.

* * *

## The Butterfly

*Characters: 2 persons and a butterfly*

**Character 1,** *holding a butterfly:* Look, I found a butterfly. Isn't it beautiful?

**Character 2:** Did you see where it came from?

**Character 1:** That flower over there.

**Character 2:** No, I mean before it landed on that flower. Where did it come from?

**Character 1:** I don't know. A butterfly house?

**Character 2:** Well, yes, I suppose you could call it a butterfly house. It came from a cocoon. Butterflies must break free of a cocoon to be able to fly.

**Character 1:** I didn't know that. How does it get into the cocoon?

**Character 2:** Butterflies don't start out looking like butterflies. They're not like baby birds that already have wings and simply grow up enough to learn to fly. Butterflies begin as an insect that looks like a worm. It's called a caterpillar.

**Character 1:** Something this beautiful was once an ugly worm?

**Character 2:** Yes. God created a plain-looking caterpillar that becomes a beautiful butterfly to remind us of how His love can change our lives. We live in a cocoon of sin, but once we come to know God's love, He sets us free and makes us beautiful so other people can see how He changed us.

**Character 1:** Isn't God's love wonderful?

* * *

## Light of the World

*Characters: Boy and Girl*

**Boy**: I was just reading something here in my Bible.  Jesus told his friends to be a light in the world.  How can a person be a light?

**Girl**: Well, let's think about the kind of lights they had in Jesus' day.  A lamp in Jesus' day was filled with oil, and then a wick was put in it. People would light the wick, and the lamp would burn for hours, until the oil ran out.

**Boy**: And, you couldn't leave the lamp alone for hours at a time. The wick had to be trimmed or else it would burn out. So throughout the day and night, they had to check the lamp and make sure the wick was trimmed. Also, they had to carry the lamp very carefully, or else the oil would spill out of the top.

**Girl**: People had to be very careful, and pay attention to their lamps in order for the lamps to keep on shining and giving off light. In the same way, we have to be careful to keep our light for Jesus shining in our lives. Just like people had to refill the oil in their lamp to keep it burning, we have to refill ourselves with God's love all the time.

**Boy**: How can we do that?

**Girl**: Well, we do it by loving other people, praying, reading the Bible, coming to church, doing nice things for other people.

**Boy**:  I get it. And just like people had to pay attention to their wick and keep it trimmed, we have to pay attention to our lives. If we love God and obey him, and love other people, we can be a light in the world.

* * *

## A Boy Named Cornelius

*Characters: Boy and his Grandfather*

**Cornelius:**  Grandfather, I hate my name. Cornelius.  It sounds dumb and the kids at school tease me about it all the time.

**Grandfather:**  It's a noble name, a Latin name. A very old name. You should be proud of it.

**Cornelius:**  That doesn't mean it's a likable name.  Why couldn't I have been named 'Jake' or 'Michael' or 'Ryan' or 'Thomas.' Anything would have been better.

**Grandfather:** But you're a special person and you have a special name.  Let me tell you about another Cornelius.  He was a Roman soldier living in a foreign land.  But he was different from the others. Not because of his name. Cornelius believed in God, the one, true God, not the many gods the other Romans believed in.  He couldn't be friends with the other Roman soldiers because of his beliefs, and he couldn't be friends with the local people because they weren't permitted to be friends with Romans.

**Cornelius:**  So if he didn't have any friends, what did he do?

**Grandfather:** Nothing, at first.  But, God did something in his life.  God sent an angel to tell Cornelius to invite a man named Peter to dinner. Cornelius wondered if Peter would actually come, since Peter was not supposed to eat dinner with a Roman.

**Cornelius:** So, how did Cornelius convince Peter to come to dinner?"

**Grandfather:** God knew that Peter would refuse the invitation and sent a dream to Peter.  In the dream, Peter saw a sheet being lowered from heaven and in the sheet were animals of all sorts. A voice told Peter to kill and eat the animals. Peter was horrified and replied that he couldn't do that because some of the animals were unacceptable to Hebrews and not to be eaten. The voice reassured Peter that he should eat them because it was God's plan. Peter was very disturbed by the dream and spent all morning trying to figure out what it meant. Then, Cornelius' messenger showed up to invite Peter to dinner. An angel explained to Peter that the dream meant Peter should eat at the Roman's house. Peter went to Cornelius' house and had dinner and began to tell Cornelius about Jesus. Then, Cornelius believed in Jesus and asked Peter to baptize him and his whole family. Peter suddenly understood the real meaning of his dream. The promise of salvation through believing in Jesus is open to Romans and all people.

**Cornelius:** So, Cornelius was a really important person then?"

**Grandfather:** Yes, Cornelius was important because he believed in God, even when it wasn't a popular choice, and God used him to teach Peter that the promise of salvation is open to all people. You might even say that Cornelius played a part in your knowing about Jesus."

**Cornelius:** Maybe it's not such a bad name after all.

\* \* \*

# Games

Playing games can reinforce a lesson, or simply be a fun way to interact with children. You don't have to think all the way back to your own childhood to remember the games you played. Many of them are listed here.

### Animal Charades
Supplies: Cards with pictures of animals (can be homemade with pictures glued to an index card)

Directions: Children sit in a circle. One selects a card and must mimic animal, with or without sound, while the others guess the animal's identity.

## Animal Concentration
Supplies: Same cards as above but be sure to have two identical of each animal
Directions: Lay the cards picture down and have the child turn over cards one at a time. Object is to try to match cards by remembering where the matches were.

## Animal Follow the Leader
Directions: the Leader acts like an animal and all the children follow mimicking him. For example, the leader might choose to be an elephant and hang his arm down as a trunk and lumber around the room. Students follow. They can guess what animal and then the Leader changes to another animal.

## Bandana Tag:
Supplies: Two bandanas per person
Directions: Tuck two bandanas into the back of each person's waistband. The object is to "tag" by snatching someone's bandana. If you lose both of yours, you must sit on the ground. But you can get back into the game by taking someone else's bandana as they run past you.

## Blind Man's Bluff:
Supplies: Blindfold
Directions: One child is blindfolded and turned three times in a circle. The other children stand near and call to him. When he moves in the direction to try to catch one, the other children call him to confuse and distract him. There are two versions: the children may move away from the blind man or they must remain in their places. When the blind man catches one, he is the next blind man.

## Chain Tag

Directions: Select two kids to be "it." Once they tag a person, they must hold their hand, by the end of the games there are two long lines of children chasing one or two kids.

## Cotton Ball Soccer
Supplies: Cotton Balls, table top
Directions: Two players stand on either side or end of a table. The cotton ball is dropped in the middle and they try to blow it to the other's end.

## Duck, Duck, Goose (Pato, Pato, Ganso)
Directions: Children sit on the floor in a circle. One child is "it" and walks the circle around behind the others, touching each one's head and saying "Duck." (or whatever word you want to use.) At some point, "it" changes to "Goose." Then "it" races around the circle chased by the "Goose." If "it" reaches the empty seat first he takes it and the "Goose" is "it" and the game continues. If the "Goose" catches up to "it" and tags him, "it" continues the game.

## Fox and Hen:
Psalm 36:7 *"How precious is your loving kindness, O God. Therefore, the children of men put their trust under the shadow of your wings.*
Directions: All but two children are baby chicks. One of the remaining two is the Hen and the other, the Fox. Object of the game is for the fox to steal all the baby chicks from the hen. The chicks line up with each one hold the waist of the one in front and "peeping." The mother hen stands in front of them and spreads her wings (arms) to protect them from the fox. She "clucks" to remind her chicks to stay behind her and attached to one another. The fox is in front of her and runs toward her to try to snatch a baby chick from the back of the line. The hen spreads her wings and moves to try to stop the fox. When she moves, the train of chicks should follow her. When the fox is able to snatch all the chicks, the game ends.

**Freeze Tag:**   *We are "frozen" in sin without Jesus to free us*

Directions: One child is "it." Whenever he catches another child and tags him, that child must "freeze" and cannot move until a child who hasn't been frozen tags him. The game continues until all children except "it" are frozen. You can also play the game with no "unfreezing" allowed.

**Fruit Basket:**
Supplies: chairs.
Directions: Every three children are named a fruit such as oranges, pears and peaches all the way around the circle. One person is "it" and does not have a seat. He calls out one or more of the fruits and those kids have to find a different seat, not the one they just vacated, before it gets to a seat. Whoever is left out is now "it." If he says "fruit basket" everyone has to change seats.

**Ha**
Directions: Have the kids lie down on the ground, each child putting his head on the next child's tummy. (The first child won't have anyone to rest their head on.) You should have a long line of kids stacked on each other's tummy in a long line. Now, starting at the top, the first child says "Ha". The second one, "Ha ha". The third one, "Ha ha ha" and so on. By the time they get to 5 or 6, you'll have a giggly bunch of kids.

**Hide the Button**
Supplies: Button or coin
Directions: Send one child from the room. Give the coin or button to one child and have him hold it in his fist behind his back. Instruct everyone to make fists and hold them behind their backs. Call the child back to the room. Tell him he has three guesses to find the coin or button. As he walks around the room, the children may help

him by saying "cold" if he walks away from the button, "warm" if he walks closer to the button. If he correctly guesses which child has the button and in which hand, the button holder leaves the room and a new child hides the button.

**If you love me, honey, you must smile  (Si usted ama mí, la miel, usted debe sonreír)**
Directions:   Kids sit in a circle, one is "it." "It" goes up to a "victim" and says "If you love me, honey, you must smile." If that person smiles, he's now "it." If he doesn't smile, "it" must find another victim. One big rule is that they're not allowed to touch the other child.

**Operator**
Directions: Sit the kids in a circle. One child thinks of a sentence to whisper in another child's ear. As it goes around the circle, the phrase may sound strange or silly, but they must pass it on exactly as they hear it. This illustrates how gossip can get twisted. If you have an English-speaking person in the circle to really throw off the phrase, they'll giggle themselves silly.

**Puzzle Race:**
Supplies:   Draw a picture on cardboard and cut into puzzle pieces
Directions:   Give each child a piece to the puzzle.  Don't tell them what the picture looks like. At the signal, the must race across the room and assemble the puzzle and figure out what the picture is.

**Rainbow Hunt Puzzle**
Supplies:  Construction paper, scissors, poster putty or tape
Directions:   Cut out a rainbow with different colors for the arc (Hint: each piece of the arc will be a different size so that they fit together with decreasing sizes), a sun and a couple rain drops.  In advance, without the children seeing you, hang the pieces in different places, using tape or poster putty.  Send the children on a scavenger hunt to find all the pieces of the rainbow, and have them assemble them.  Can make two sets and have a race to see which team can find and assemble first.

**Red Rover**
Directions:  Divide the kids into two teams.  Each team lines up, arms locked together shoulder to shoulder facing the other

team. The first team calls out, "Red Rover, Red Rover, we dare Jose to come over!" Jose then has to run across to the taunting team and try to "break" through the locked arms. If he succeeds he gets to take one person from the taunting team back to his team with him and then the other team gets its turn. If he loses he has to join the taunting team.

## Simon Says:

Directions: One child is "Simon" and stands facing the other children. Whatever he tells the students, they must do, but only if he says "Simon says" first. He can trick them by doing the activity with them, but without the "Simon says" tag. If the student des the activity when he's not supposed to, he's out of the game. Examples: "Simon says jump up and down," "Simon says put one hand on your head," "Simon says stick out your tongue," "Hold up you right hand." Anyone who held up their right hand is out.

## Snatch

Supplies: Assorted objects
Directions: Put 12-20 assorted small items on a table. Let the children study them for a minute. Then instruct them to turn around and close their eyes. Remove one item and shuffle the others. When the children turn around and open their eyes, they must guess what's missing.

## String Game:

We are all brothers and sisters in God's eyes.
Supplies: A ball of string or twine.
Directions: Have everyone stand in a circle. One person is holding the ball of string. As he holds the end of the string, he chooses someone on the opposite side of the circle and says, "You (Name of the child, if possible) are my brother (sister)." Then he tosses the ball to that person, being sure to hold onto the end of the string as he does so. The two are now attached to the string. The child with the ball does the same thing, holding onto a piece of the string as he tosses the ball to another child and says, "You are my brother (sister)." When all children have gotten and tossed the ball, a web should be

formed in the middle of the circle, illustrating how we are all connected to God as his children and to each other through his love.

### Tigger Tag
Directions:The kids are all tiggers and one is the tigger catcher. Everyone has to bounce. Instead of counting, say "Go, Tiggers, Go!"

### Turtle behind the Rock
Supplies: An umbrella or large box or sheet
Directions: Send one child from the room, have everyone else change seats. One child hides under the umbrella, box or sheet. The child who returns has ten seconds to guess who is missing.

* * *

# Crafts

Again, simplicity is the key to success. Try to tie in the craft with the lesson, and make it repeatable so that the teacher can reproduce it with the supplies she has available to her.

You can purchase 4 inch by 6 inch cards which, when cut in half lengthwise, are perfect for making bookmarks. Use stamps or stickers to decorate them, punch a hole and thread through a piece of yarn. You can also print the lesson theme or a Bible verse on the bookmark.

Use wooden clothes pins as a base for several projects. Glue on a butterfly, or sticker and clip them onto the child's clothing for a quick and easy craft. White paper plates can be decorated as a wreath for any holiday or cut in half and colored as a rainbow. You can glue a coloring page to the center because the plate will make the project last longer in little hands.

## Animal Mobile
Supplies: Animal pictures (see games section), string or yarn, unsharpened pencil, scissors, glue or glue stick, construction paper
Directions: Have students cut our animal pictures and glue to construction paper. After glue has dried, cut out the construction paper, glue end of string or yarn to the back and tie around a pencil. Use varying lengths of yarn or string.

## Butterflies (Mariposas)
Supplies: Craft Foam, scissors, clothes pins, pipe cleaners, glue, glitter
Directions: Glue butterfly to clothes pin. Add pipe cleaner antennae. Decorate with glitter.

## Butterfly Bookmarks
Supplies: Card Stock, stamps, stamp pads, glitter, marker
Directions: Stamp butterfly on card stock. Write verse (En Cristo somos nuevas personas) or child's name with marker. Decorate with glitter.

## Caterpillar and Cocoon
II Corinthians 5:17  "...if anyone is in Christ, he is a new creation; the old has gone and the new has come."
Supplies: Construction paper, pipe cleaners, scissors, glue (or glue stick), pencil
Directions: Draw a caterpillar on construction paper and cut out or make a caterpillar from a pipe cleaner folded in half and twisted. Draw the cocoon on brown construction paper, cut out both pieces and glue the edges together, leaving the top open so that a pocket is formed. Cut out a butterfly from another piece of construction paper. Fold in half and tuck into the cocoon (after glue has dried). Describe how a caterpillar forms a cocoon and tuck your pipe cleaner caterpillar into the cocoon. Read the verse above and pull out the butterfly.

## Chains of Love
Supplies: construction paper, pen, scissors, tape or stapler

Directions: Cut paper into 2" x ½" strips. Write "love" (amor) on each strip, loop into a circle with the word on the outside and fasten with tape or staple. Feed the next strip through the first loop and fasten it to make a chain. Alternate colors of paper any way you wish. You can also put the child's name on the inside of the strip.

## Christmas Card Mobile
Supplies: Christmas Cards, string or yarn, pencils, hole punch
Directions: Cut shapes and pictures from the front of Christmas Cards, punch holes and string them one from another from a pencil.

## Coffee Filter Butterflies
Supplies: Paper coffee filters, pipe cleaners, markers, water, optional glue, glitter
Directions: Color filter with several different markers. Sprinkle a filter lightly with water to encourage the colors to run together. (Or, use glitter and glue for s special effect.) When the colors dry, pinch the center of the filter like a bow tie and use a pipe cleaner to form the body of the butterfly, the ends of the pipe cleaner form antennae. Fan out the sides of the filter for wings.

## Fingerprint Bugs
Supplies: Paper, ink stamp pad (hint-use washable ink), hand-wipe or liquid soap and paper towel, marking pen
Directions: Press finger tip to stamp pad and then to paper. With marking pen, add antennae and you may also draw wings for different types of bugs. Hand-wipe or soap and towel for cleaning ink from hand.

## Hand-print Chain
We are all connected through God's love
Supplies: construction paper, pen, scissors, tape or stapler
Directions: Trace child's hand on paper and cut it out. Write child's name on his paper hand. Attach hands thumb to thumb, or fifth finger to fifth finger with tape or staple until a chain is made.

## Heart-Lacing Project
Supplies: Construction paper, scissors, hole punch, yarn
Directions: Cut a heart out of the construction paper. Punch holes ½ inch in from the edge. Thread a piece of yarn so that it ties in a bow at the bottom of the heart. Let the children decorate the heart and thread the yarn.

## Joseph and the Coat of Many Colors
Supplies: Craft pipe cleaners in colors, pen, white craft glue, doll hair or yarn (if desired), brown lunch bags, scissors
Directions: Cut pipe cleaners in half. Assemble different colors on the side of an unopened lunch bag and glue in place. Draw head and glue hair or yarn for hair. Draw a face. Use pipe cleaners for arms and a shepherd's crook.

## Paper Plate Fish
Supplies: white paper plates with the ruffled edges, scissors, glue, crayons
Directions: Cut a pie-shaped wedge out of a paper plate. The wedge will be the fish's tail; the hole will be the fish's mouth. Glue the wedge on the edge opposite the "mouth" and decorate.

## Paper Plate Wreath
Supplies:　white paper plates with the ruffled edges, construction paper, pencil, scissors, glue or gluestick, hole punch, yarn, stickers, glitter
Directions: Decorate for a holiday, punch a hole in the top and thread with yarn to hang. For a hands wreath, trace hands on paper and cut out, lay along the outer edge of the plate, palms slightly overlapping. Glue in place. Punch a hole in the top and hang with yarn.

## Pipe Cleaner Animals
Supplies: Craft pipe cleaners in colors, eyes, mini-pompoms, white craft glue
Directions: Cut two pipe cleaners of the same color in half. Twist to form legs and bend the tips to form feet. Use a whole pipe cleaner for body, neck and head—bending the tip for the head. Cut another ½ pipe cleaner in half again and use it for a tail. Decorate with eyes or pompoms if desired.

## Praise Streamers
Supplies: Weaving loops, ribbon, scissors
Directions: Cut 3' lengths of ribbon and secure to the loop. Hold loop in hand or around wrist and dance to praise music.

## Rainbow Mobile
Supplies: Unsharpened pencils, string, construction paper, scissors, tape or glue
Directions: Cut appropriately colored construction paper into these shapes: ½ circle (sun), raindrop, arcs of a rainbow. Tape or glue end of a short piece of string to the sun, medium length string to one or two rain drops and longer, varying lengths to each arc of color for the rainbow. Tie other ends to the pencil with sun near the eraser, raindrops next and rainbow on the left side. To make a rainbow, the sun must shine through raindrops.

# Puppets

Children everywhere love puppets. We take a dozen small hand puppets with us and let the children participate in impromptu puppet shows, sometime as simple as "dancing" while we sing songs. Paper bag or sock puppets are simple to make and can even be part of the crafts.

## Sock Puppets
Supplies:    Socks (adult sized, any color, works best for Adults' hands), Yarn, buttons, thread and a needle, scissors Red felt, glue (optional)

Directions: Insert hand into sock. Tuck part of the sock between your thumb and palm for the "mouth." Sew or glue buttons for eyes (where your knuckles are). Sew or glue yarn for hair (on the back of your hand). Optional: cut a piece of red felt for inside of mouth and sew or glue in the appropriate place. You can also decorate the puppet with a scarf or bow tie around the neck (your wrist).

### Puppet Screen

For a simple puppet screen, use an extendable curtain tension rod set in a doorway or between the backs of two chairs. Thread an inexpensive curtain or scrap of fabric over it.

For the best results with puppet shows, pre-record the script and play the tape while manipulating the puppets. Be sure to add music at the beginning and end of the show!

## Felt Board

You can make a simple and portable felt board to illustrate stories. For the "characters," you can photocopy pictures from a book, cut them and glue to a piece of cardboard. Add a dot of Velcro® so the picture will stick to the felt.

## Making a Simple and Portable Felt Board

Supplies: 2 pieces of 12 inch x 12 inch heavy cardboard—(Hint: the size and kind of cardboard that comes with photo album/scrapbooks)
> Scraps of felt—blue, white, green
> Velcro®
> Hole punch
> Pieces of yarn or string
> Pictures
> Cardboard, lighter weight such as poster board
> Craft or Fabric Glue

Glue felt scraps to two pieces of heavy cardboard. Dark blue can be water; cut it with waves on the surface and cover the lower half of one piece. Lighter blue or white can be the sky. You can add a half-circle yellow sun if you want. On the other piece of cardboard, glue green on the lower half for earth and white above it for sky. You can add a tree or hills or a river to the earth scene.

On the lighter weight cardboard, glue pictures of people, animals. Cut pieces in the shape of a boat, basket, tent, house, etc. and color or decorate them. On the back of each piece, glue a small piece of Velcro.

Punch three holes across the top of each board. Holding them with the felt sides facing each other, thread a small piece of yarn or string through one pair of holes and tie a bow, repeat with all holes. The boards now form an easel. Turn them with the felt sides out and you have your "stage." Turn them with the felt sides facing and you can easily pack them in a box or suitcase.

Use the board to illustrate any story. Put the pictures together in zippered-closure plastic bags so that when you want to tell a story, you don't have to sort through all pictures for the right ones.

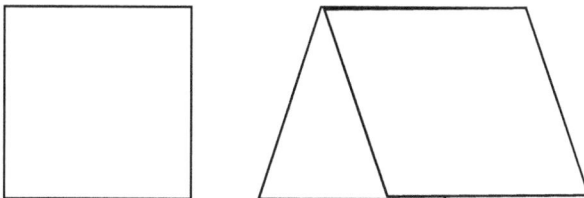

\* \* \*

## Action Plan

### Personal response:
Plan your Visiting Bible School lessons, activities and crafts.

### Awareness:
Allow plenty of time during your trip preparations for team members to become familiar with the crafts and activities.

### Making a Difference:
Expect great things to come from your VBS for the children, their teachers and your team.

# Who Am I that I Should Go?

# Chapter 20

## Leading a Medical Mission Team

*Jesus knew in his spirit what they were thinking in their hearts, and he said to them, "Why are you thinking these things? Which is easier to say to the paralytic, 'Your sins are forgiven, or get up, take your mat and walk?' But that you may know that the Son of Man has authority on earth to forgive sins." He said to the paralytic, "I tell you, get up, take your mat and go home."*
Mark 2: 8-11

A Short-Term Medical Mission offers a model of living a holistic Gospel message by providing compassion, mercy and care to the whole person. As with all types of Short-Term Mission teams, the medical mission is about people, not programs, facilities, plans, or medical care. By its nature, a Medical Mission Team is people-oriented. However, it is easy to fall into attitudes that separate the team from the people they have come to serve, such as:

- Emphasizing the numbers of people treated each day;
- Moving people through the clinic as quickly as possible;
- Counting how many toothbrushes are distributed;
- Believing Western medicine is always superior to their ways;
- Failing to recognize that illness impacts the whole person— body, mind and spirit.

## A New Model for Delivery of Healthcare

A medical mission differs from the care most professionals deliver in their daily work.

| Traditional, Secular Model | Community-Based Primary Care |
|---|---|
| 1. Efficient, effective, outcome-oriented medical care is the primary goal. | 1. The primary goal is establishing relationships in which God's love can be shared in practical ways. |
| 2. Emphasizes technology, equipment, procedures and medications. | 2. Emphasizes people, using appropriate, available & self-sustaining technology. |
| 3. The Western physician "takes over." | 3. The Western physician learns and teaches. |
| 4. The team brings answers and solutions to problems. | 4. The team encourages empowerment of local people to solve their own problems. |
| 5. Authority comes from knowledge, skills and experience. | 5. Authority comes from God, and is demonstrated in humility and service to others. |

## Planning and Preparation

The composition of a Medical Mission Team mixes professionals, physicians, dentists, nurses, medical assistants, therapists, pharmacists, technicians and phlebotomists, and lay people. As you begin to recruit team members, plan for one-to-two persons to work with each physician or dentist. Assigning a nurse to each physician works well, because nurses understand medical jargon and can translate it for patients and other team members. A second person can assist with the actual examination, or hold babies while the parent is being examined. Often, this person is also a translator.

In the absence of a pharmacist, a nurse can manage the pharmacy, under the direction of a physician. Lay persons can assist with clerical duties, check vital signs, conduct vision exams for reading glasses, assist doctors, fill medication bottles, escort patients, and entertain children.

Medical personnel may have to work outside their specialties. However, this can also be a welcomed challenge. Doing something different, without the pressures of meeting productivity levels, the hassles of dealing with paperwork and insurance forms, can actually be refreshing.

Prior to her first Medical Mission, a geriatrics specialist worried about handling pediatrics in the clinic. Within a few hours of her first day there, she had seen her first case of mumps, treated a six-year-old with pneumonia, and examined an adolescent with a fractured hip.

"It all comes back to you," she said, reminiscing about her training years.

A dentist had similar feelings about how different a medical mission was, compared with his usual practice. He reported he had extracted more teeth in one week than he had in twenty years of work.

People with no medical background enjoy the opportunity to learn new skills. On our medical team, a mechanical engineer checks temperatures and blood pressures, a librarian conducts vision examinations, a student nurse assists the dentist, and a secretary works in the pharmacy.

## White Coats

What should your medical team members wear? Many feel comfortable in scrubs, and these are easy to wear and launder in most circumstances. However, if your team is traveling by boat to a remote village, then sloshing through mud, or squatting in the dirt to examine a patient, jeans might be a better choice. The shoes (clogs) preferred by many medical personnel may also not be the best choice. Ask you host what to expect of the terrain and climate when making footwear choices. For the jungle, hiking boots might be best. Scrubs might not be appropriate in certain places where the team's safety coming and going might be jeopardized by being readily identified as medical personnel.

If your team members do plan to wear scrubs, check with a hospital laundry company to see if they could donate any for your use.

Scrub jackets are often a better choice than white lab coats which intimidate some people. Children may already be shy with strangers, especially those of a different race and culture. Consider wearing something child friendly, if you can. (The pockets of a scrub jacket also make a handy place to carry a small puppet along with your medical equipment.)

## Supplies

The medical supplies you will need can vary according to the type of care provided or the target population served. The in-country hosts can advise you on the specific needs of the community, common illnesses, and the ages of the people you will treat. Because of the limitations of providing follow-up and long-term monitoring, you may not be able to treat chronic conditions such as diabetes or hypertension.

Whenever possible, ask for donations of supplies. Physicians' offices may seem like a good place to ask, however, the medications they receive as samples are usually not what you want. They often have excessive packaging because they are not supposed to be a month's supply, but a few days of sampling.

Always check expiration dates. If you bring expired medications, Customs officials can confiscate them and possible all of your supplies.

251

Add to your team paperwork, a Letter of Intent and a Bill of Laden, to prevent many problems. The Letter of Intent, written in both English and the language of the country you are visiting, indicates the medications will be dispensed under the auspices of the sponsoring organization and not sold. The sponsoring organization should provide this to you. Give team members a copy of the letter to carry in their suitcases.

The Bill of Laden lists the medications, quantities, and their values for Customs Officials. Your host may want a copy of this in advance.

## Pharmacy

Either a pharmacist, a nurse (under the direction of a physician) can manage a pharmacy. I create a Medication Book for the pharmacy and each physician and dentist. A page for each medication with brand and generic names, indications for use, side effects and a table of appropriate dosages give immediate information for the practitioner. You can color code the pages according to the type of medication: antibiotic, analgesic, anti-fungal, etc.

In the front of the book, list all of the meds including how many doses are available. The pharmacy personnel can update this list every day so that the physicians know when supplies are running low and what alternatives are still available.

You can often pre-pack most medications in the appropriate dosage, for example, twenty-one pills of a medication that is given three times per day for seven days. Label the bottles exactly as a pharmacy would do, and preferably, in the language of your patients. A translator should also go over the instructions with the patient. Use containers with child-safety lids instead of plastic bags, if possible.

Keep in mind as you write or offer directions that when a medication is ordered three times a day, you might suggest breakfast, lunch and dinner times, but your patients might not eat three meals a day. Suggesting specific times might not work well with people who do not have a clock. Instead, you might say, "morning," "afternoon," or "evening."

## Suggested List of Pharmacy Supplies and Medications

- □ Alcohol gel and alcohol pads
- □ Scissors
- □ Clean, empty pill bottles
- □ Vinyl gloves
- □ Pill cutter
- □ Cotton Balls (dispense with ear drops)
- □ Medicine cups (or small paper cups)
- □ Extra pre-printed and blank labels
- □ Pill tray and spatula for counting
- □ Paper towels
- □ Small funnel (for pouring powdered meds into bottles)
- □ Plastic trash bags
- □ Child medicine spoons (dispense with liquid medications)
- □ Gallon-sized, zippered-closure plastic bags (for all of the bottles of one family)
- □ Fine-tipped permanent markers to write the patient's name on bags or bottles
- □ Bottled water to mix powdered meds and ORS
- □ Prenatal & children's vitamins
- □ Analgesics (aspirin, acetaminophen, & ibuprofen) for adults & children
- □ Cold medications, cough syrup, & throat lozenges
- □ Eye drops (medicated & saline)
- □ Ear drops (antibiotic & analgesic)
- □ Skin rash creams, antibiotic & anti-fungal creams
- □ Hydrocortisone cream
- □ Diaper rash creams & petroleum jelly
- □ Treatments for scabies & lice
- □ Antibiotics
- □ Anti-fungal medication
- □ Anti-amebics
- □ Anti-diarrheals
- □ Antihistamines

## Purchasing Medications

Several companies supply medications for mission teams, for either a fixed donation or purchased at great discount. All of the companies require your team to be affiliated with a non-profit organization. Some companies require a copy of the license of a medical professional on your team. The companies may also request a follow-up report after your mission trip describing how the medications were used and how you handled any leftover drugs.

## Sources for Medications and Supplies

- AmeriCares, www.americares.org/
  AmeriCares is an international relief
  organization

- Blessings International, www.blessing.org
  Blessings Internaitonal is a source of
  pharmaceuticals, vitamins, & medical
  supplies for clinics, hospitals & Short-Term
  Missions

- CrossLink International,
  www.crosslinkinternational.net
  CrossLink supplies Medical Mission
  Teams, humanitarian aid organizations,
  free clinics & hospitals

- Map International, www.map.org
  The MAP Travel Pack® is a pre-packed
  assortment of medicines and other general
  medical supplies

## ORS versus Sports Drinks

Oral Re-hydration Solution (ORS) is a simple and life-saving formula you can purchase or make. You can buy the packets and mix it into bottled water. One bottle can be given to the patient immediately and a second one sent home with instructions to drink it later that day or the next. (See the recipe for ORS in Chapter 12.)

**Do not mistake electrolyte-replenishment drinks (sports drinks) for ORS.** For team members, who are otherwise healthy individuals, sports drinks, powdered lemonade, etc., are appropriate for use during bouts of simple diarrhea. For infants and children, already on the edge of malnutrition, these beverages do not have the nutrients they need.

## Gentian Violet

Many physicians are not familiar with this inexpensive and valuable anti-fungal medication. Gentian Violet is an effective treament for:

- Serious thermal burns
- Skin and gum infections
- Vaginal yeast infections
- Thrush infections.

If a nursing baby has thrush, the mother should apply Gentian Violet to her nipples and, using a cotton-tip applicator, dab it on any white patches in the baby's mouth. Usually, only one application is necessary to clear up the infection. Gentian Violet does not require a doctor's prescription, but you may need to ask the pharmacist for it as it may be difficult to find. Purchase two bottles. You can pour a small amount into a separate bottle to dispense to a patient. Give several cotton-tip applicators to use to paint it onto the infected area. One caution: it is a purple dye and does not wash off skin, mucus membranes, clothing or surfaces.

## Medical Supplies

The type of Medical Mission (relief or development) will determibne the types of supplies you will need. **Relief** (usually following a disaster of some sort) involves emergent care. Patients can be expected to have accident-associated injuries, such as fractures, burns, lacerations, and trauma. Surgical and emergency first-aid will be your primary types of care.

With community-based primary care in a **development** environment, patients are more likely to have sub-acute illnesses such as eye, ear, upper respiratory, skin, and parasitic intestinal infections, and need Well-Baby and routine OB-Gyn care.

## Consent and Privacy

One of the greatest surprises to most medical professionals on their first Short-Term Mission trip is the absence of familiar paperwork regarding consent and privacy. Children may be brought for treament by a relative, other than parents, by a neighbor, or by a teacher or childcare worker. Sometimes, the person bringing a group of children doesn't even know their names and ages.

Should you provide them care? Yes, but try not to send medications home with children unless there is an adult you can instruct. Discuss with your host any concerns about treating children without their parents present.

Privacy can be difficult to maintain when you have little more than a tarp dividing areas of the clinic. We have held a blanket up as a screen for an examination. Check with your local host about cultural requirements for gynecological and female breast examinations, and prostate checks. Will you need a female physician or nurse-practitioner to examine women?

## Suggested List of General Medical Supplies

| Relief Medical Care | Development Medical Care |
| --- | --- |
| ☐ Alcohol gel & alcohol pads | ☐ Alcohol gel & alcohol pads |
| ☐ 4x4 & 2x2 gauze squares | ☐ 2x2 gauze squares for dental use |
| ☐ Adhesive bandages, Liquid Bandage® | ☐ Adhesive bandages, Liquid Bandage® |
| ☐ Butterflies® & Steristrips® | ☐ Butterflies® & Steristrips® |
| ☐ Gauze rolls | ☐ Tape, different sizes & types |
| ☐ Elastic wraps, 3-inch, 4-inch & 6-inch | ☐ Cotton-tip applicators & tongue blades |
| ☐ Eye pads & shields | ☐ Cotton Balls |
| ☐ Splints & plaster for casts | ☐ Bandage scissors & forceps |
| ☐ Tape, different sizes & types | ☐ Suture removal scissors & forceps |
| ☐ Cotton-tip applicators & tongue blades | ☐ Exam Gloves (latex or vinyl) |
| ☐ Cotton Balls | ☐ Digital thermometers, or ear thermometers |
| ☐ Bandage scissors & forceps | ☐ Stethoscope |
| ☐ Sutures & suture kits | ☐ Fetal stethoscope |
| ☐ Suture removal scissors and forceps | ☐ BP cuff (adult & pediatric) |
| ☐ Exam & sterile gloves ((latex or vinyl) | ☐ Otoscope & Opthalmoscope |
| ☐ Digital thermometers, or ear thermometers | ☐ Penlight |
| ☐ Stethoscope | ☐ Vaginal Speculum |
| ☐ BP cuffs (adult and pediatric) | |
| ☐ Otoscope & Opthalmoscope | |
| ☐ Penlight | |
| ☐ Portable nebulizer | |
| ☐ IV supplies | |
| ☐ Syringes & needles for local anesthesia | |

# Traffic Flow

As you plan a clinic, consider the traffic flow. You can establish a pattern even if you don't know the layout of the facility. You will need a waiting area either outside, or inside near the entrance. Post one or two local people at the door to assist with crowd control and security.

Be sure to allow plenty of room for children, and, if possible, some activity to keep them entertained. Coloring books and crayons work well. Dump several boxes of crayons into a gallon-sized plastic bag and allow them to share the bag. The waiting area is also an excellent place to provide healthcare education. Hang posters, if you can. Use simple materials with pictures and very few words to offer instructions about topics such as hand-washing and teeth-brushing.

From the waiting area, patients stop first at a registration table to begin History & Physical forms which they carry to each subsequent station. Use local help or a translator at the registration desk to begin the paperwork. The next stop is a scale and tape measure (taped to the wall) where the patient's height and weight are recorded on the form. The patient proceeds to the next station where the temperature and pulse are checked for all patients, but only adults need to have blood pressure checked. The team members working in these areas may learn enough of the local language to manage their jobs, or have printed cards with the phrases they will need.

The first available physician examines patients. If a gynecological examination is needed, set aside a curtained corner of the clinic for greater privacy. Your host can advise you whether you will need a female physician or nurse pracitioner for these examinations. Physicians and dentists who do not speak the local language will need translators. Each physician might have a nurse to assist, and a dentist needs a "chairside" assistant and, perhaps, a second person to hold a flashlight.

The dentist cannot keep up with the physicians in terms of caseload. Fortunately, not every patient requires a dental exam. The physician may "refer" those patients who do need to see the dentist. Both the physician and dentist will write prescriptions for medications to be dispensed by the pharmacy.

The final stop for every patient is the pharmacy where patients turn in their forms, pick up prescription medications, treatment for parasites (if ordered), vitamins, a toothbrush and toothpaste, and instructions how to take their medications. The pharmacy area also needs an interpreter. When you set up a pharmacy area, try to use a corner out of the way, and near the exit, where you can control the flow of traffic and secure the medications as much as possible.

**Suggested Clinic Flow Chart**

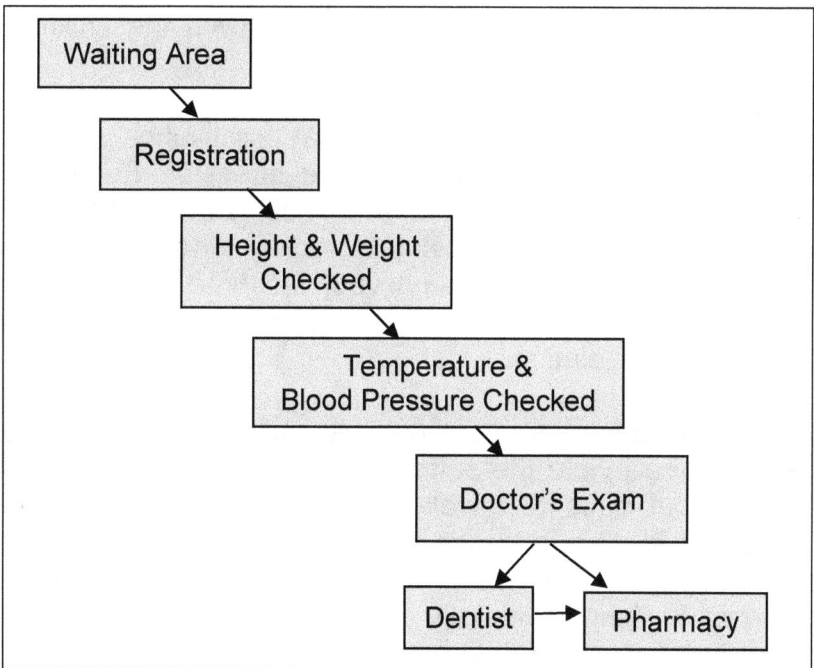

## Team Leader

Create a daily schedule of staffing. Team members may want to rotate responsibilities throughout the week and work with different people, if possible. On a recent medical team, two nurses volunteered to set up the pharmacy and staff it all week, rather than rotate. They ran the best and most efficient pharmacy we have ever had.

If you have sufficient personnel, assign one or more person to "float" between areas, providing breaks, making sure team members have plenty of water, escorting patients, holding babies, and providing an extra pair of hands wherever needed. As team leader, try not to tie yourself down so that you are available when questions or problems arise, or to give breaks as needed.

Don't forget your Visiting Bible School, if you are having one. Medical personnel love to have an opportunity to get away from the clinic for a few minutes and interact with the children in VBS. Try to schedule that into the day.

No matter how experienced a medical practitioner is, working with a medical mission team can be stressful. Supplies are often scarce, diseases unusual, and patients living in desperate situations. Burnout can accelerate rapidly when coupled with culture shock. Keep an eye on your first-time team members and be prepared to give them a hand or a break if the work becomes overwhelming.

We often encounter tragic situations and the care we have to offer cannot alleviate the suffering or solve the problem. Maria came into our clinic for a well-child checkup. She is an 8-year-old blind child who, had she been treated eariler, might have some vision now. Fourteen-year-old Anna revealed to a nurse that she is being sexually abused and has a sexually-transmitted disease. Paola brought in her six daughters under the age of six, the whole family suffering from severe malnutrition and pneumonia. We do what we can and offer what we have, but we can only do so much. Don't make promises you cannot keep. You can refer a patient to a local practitioner, but you will never know if the patient was able to keep the appointment and to afford care.

Your heart aches when you cannot "fix" situations like these. Even though you might not be able to cure every patient, you can offer prayer. Pray with patients. When you don't speak their language, your words can still bring comfort and hope. Forget about the lines waiting to see the doctor, take a few minutes to pray with patients who need this as much as they need medicine.

# Housecalls

An invitation to visit a home is one of the blessings of a medical mission. Taking a doctor, nurse, and interpreter away from the clinic for perhaps an hour or more may seem inefficient, especially when there may be fifty other people waiting to be seen. However, keep in mind, the mission is not about numbers; your goal is to meet the needs of people one-by-one.

\* \* \*

### Experiences with Housecalls

We walked down a dirt path kept plant-free by sheep grazing along the edges. About a half-mile from the clinic, we stopped at a two-story mud brick house the interpreter told us was more than 150 years old. We ducked to enter a doorway that was about five feet tall and found ourselves in a front room that had, at one time, served as a small food store. Dust-covered glass cabinets and wooden shelves lined the walls. Stalks of alfalfa, feed for guinea pigs, occupied one corner of the room, and a faded piece of cloth hung on the wall above a low wooden bench.

An elderly man greeted us, then sat on a bench, the only place to sit in the room. Dr. Stephen knelt on the dirt floor and began an examination while I wrote notes on a patient form. As we worked, I glanced out the door to see a pig wandering down the road. The patient had catarracts, and osteoarthritis, typical for a man in his eighties. We gave him some acetaminophen.

Word spread that the doctor would come to a home and another invitation came the next day. We traveled a little farther to the home of another elderly man and his wife, a Quechua healing woman. She invited us to tour her garden after we treated her husband. She identified each plant and its use. Some were familiar: foxglove, which we know as Digitalis, a heart medication, and plátano, or plantain, a good source of Vitamin C. If she had simply come to the clinic, we might never have had the opportunity to learn from her.

While leaving a bottle of anti-inflammatory medication was all we could do for either patient, our willingness to come into their homes brought the love of God to them. Yet, we were the ones blessed by the trust they showed in extending the invitations. A year later we found out that after our visit, the couple decided to visit the church that had sponsored our clinic. Medical care can be evangelistic.

\* \* \*

*"As you go, preach this message:*
*'The kingdom of heaven is near.'*
*Heal the sick, raise the dead, cleanse those*
*who have leprosy, drive out demons.*
*Freely you have received, freely give."*
Jesus' instructions to his disciples,
Matt 10: 6-8

## Action Plan

### Personal response:
Establish a Medical Team to address physical, emotional & spiritual needs.

### Awareness:
Discuss how your team can alleviate the suffering of God's people.

### Making a Difference:
Look for ways to make a difference in one person's life. Focus on ways to encourage development in the host community.

# Chapter 21

## Rashes, Fevers, and Other Infections

Many diseases rarely seen in the U.S. are common in Third World countries. Fortunately, medications that you will commonly dispense for other illnesses can be used to treat these infections.

## Parasites & Worms

| Disease | Cause | Symptoms | Treatment |
| --- | --- | --- | --- |
| **Anisakiasis** | Roundworm (nematode) | Epigastric pain, nausea, vomiting, low-grade fever, diffuse lower abdominal pain, diarrhea; chronic gastritis, peptic ulcer disease, inflammatory bowel disease | Symptomatic |
| **Ascariasis** | Roundworm (nematode) | Transient respiratory & chronic GI | Albendazole 400 mg |
| **chinococcosis** | Tapeworm | Hydatid cyst in liver, lungs | Albendazole 400 mg Surgery |
| **Enterobiasis** | Pinworm (nematode) | Perianal pruritis, secondary enuresis & urinary tract | Albendazole 400 mg |

# Who Am I that I Should Go?

| Disease | Cause | Symptoms | Treatment |
|---------|-------|----------|-----------|
| | | infection | |
| **Hookworm** | | Anemia, anorexia or increased appetite, abdominal discomfort, weight loss, nausea & vomiting, diarrhea or constipation | Albendazole 400 mg |
| **Scabies** | Mite Sarcoptes scabiei | Itching, burrows under skin, rash | Permethrin |
| **Strongylodiasis** | Roundworm (nematode) | Cutaneous inflammation, serpiginous or urticarial tracts, & pruritis; pulmonary or GI symptoms | Symptomatic |
| **Tapeworms & Cysticercosis** | Beef tapeworm (found in uncooked meat) | GI discomfort & weight loss | Symptomatic |
| **Toxocariasis** | Worms in feces-contaminated dirt | Eosinophilia, decreased immune competence, malaise, fever, cough & wheezing, hepatomegaly, anorexia, weight loss | Symptomatic |
| **Trematodes** | Fluke-contaminated water | Fever, cough, abdominal pain (especially hepatic), nausea, diarrhea, & hepatomegaly | Symptomatic |
| **Trichinosis** | Roundworm | Malaise, nausea, | Albendazole |

# Who Am I that I Should Go?

| Disease | Cause | Symptoms | Treatment |
|---|---|---|---|
| | (in uncooked meat) | cramping abdominal pain, & diarrhea; fever, eosinophilia, periorbital & facial edema, conjunctivitis, dysphagia, dyspnea, cough, myalgia, & muscle spasms | 400 mg |
| **Trichuriasis** | Roundworm | Abdominal cramping, nausea, vomiting, flatulence, diarrhea, tenesmus, & weight loss | Albendazole 400 mg |

## Protozoan Infections

| Disease | Cause | Symptoms | Treatment |
|---|---|---|---|
| **Chagas' Disease or American trypanoso-miais** | Insect bite | Fever, Tachycardia. Fatigue, weakness, Splenomegaly, Myocarditis, meningoenceph-alitis | Symptomatic |
| **Leishmaniasis** | Sandfly bite | Visceral, cutaneous, Mucocutaneous | Symptomatic |
| **Typhus (rickettsioses** | Arthropod bite or feces | Headache, high fever, chills, macular rash, petechia, delirium, Photophobia, | Symptomatic |

| Disease | Cause | Symptoms | Treatment |
|---|---|---|---|
| Giardiasis | Human feces-contaminated water | Eye pain, hearing loss, hypotension<br><br>Greasy, frothy, foul-smelling stools, N & V abdominal pain | Symptomatic |

## Bacterial and Viral Infections

| Disease | Cause | Symptoms | Treatment |
|---|---|---|---|
| **Bartonello-sis (Oroya fever)** | Gram negative bacteria transmitted by sandfly bite | Fever, malaise, headache, myalgia, chills, drenching sweats, lymphadenopathy, hemolytic anemia, liver involvement & altered consciousness. | Symptomatic |
| **Brucellosis (Malta fever)** | Bacteria in unpasteurized milk, cheese | Fever, sweating, muscle pain | Long-term antibiotics |
| **Diphtheria** | Bacterium | Fever, serosanguinous nasal discharge, sore throat, gray pharyngeal or tracheal pseudomem-brane | |
| **Impetigo** | Staph aureus, Streptococcus | Skin blisters & lesions | Gentian Violet, anti-fungals, antibiotics |
| **Pertussis (whooping cough)** | Bacterium | Slight fever, dry cough, coryza, sneezing, malaise, & anorexia; paroxysmal violent coughing spells | |

# Who Am I that I Should Go?

| Disease | Cause | Symptoms | Treatment |
|---|---|---|---|
| | | with respiratory distress & a high-pitched inspiratory crowing whoop | |
| **Rotavirus** | Rotavirus | Non-inflammatory diarrhea, gastroenteritis | Supportive |
| **Typhoid and paratyphoid fever** | Bacterium in feces-contaminated food or water | Fever, chills, malaise, headache, sore throat, cough, & abdominal pain, constipation or diarrhea. | |

# Diseases of Malnutrition

| Disease | Cause | Symptoms | Treatment |
|---|---|---|---|
| **Cachexia** | Cancer, AIDS, severe illness | Weakness, lethargy, emaciation, equal fat & muscle loss, loss of bone minerals | Treatment of underlying illness first |
| **Malabsorp-tion** | Diarrhea, metabolic disorder, chronic illness, parasitic infections | Anorexia, weight loss, malaise, failure to thrive, poor turgor, skin wrinkling | Improved nutrition, oral re-hydration solution |
| **Maras-mus** | Inadequate caloric intake | Failure to gain weight, emaciation | Improved nutrition |
| **Kwashiorkor** | Protein-calorie malnutrition | Lethargy, irritability, anorexia, weakness, loss of | Fluid, protein and calorie replacement, vitamins |

| Disease | Cause | Symptoms | Treatment |
|---|---|---|---|
| Pellagra | Lack of niacin, protein, tryptophan | muscle, edema, hair loss<br><br>Diarrhea, dermatitis, dementia, death | Niacin |

## Childhood Diseases

| Disease | Cause | Symptoms | Treatment |
|---|---|---|---|
| Chicken Pox | Varicella zoster virus | 2-4 mm papulla which becomes a vesicle, breaks open into a crusty lesion | Isolate from pregnant women, neonates; symptomatic |
| Fifth Disease | Parvovirus B19 | Red, lacy rash beginning on cheeks, spreading to body | Isolate from pregnant women; symptomatic |
| German Measles (Rubella) | Rubella virus | Low grade fever, swollen lymph glands, joint pains, headache, conjunctivitis, fine red rash | Isolate from pregnant women; symptomatic |
| Measles (Rubeola) | Paramyxo-virus | Cough, coryza & conjunctivitis, maculopapular, erythematous rash | Isolate from pregnant women; symptomatic |
| Mumps | Virus | Parotiditis, swelling of glands, orchitis, headache, fever | Acetamin-ophen (avoid aspirin) |

## Pandemic Illnesses

# Who Am I that I Should Go?

| Disease | Cause | Symptoms | Treatment |
|---------|-------|----------|-----------|
| **Influenza (Asian, Avian, Hong Kong, Spanish, Swine, Flu)** | Influenza A Virus | Chills, fever sore throat, muscle pains, severe headache, coughing, weakness | Symptomatic antiviral drugs |
| **Cholera** | Bacterium in food/water | Diarrhea, rapid dehydration, rapid pulse, dry skin, tiredness, abdominal cramps, nausea, & vomiting, sudden death | Oral Re-hydration Solution, antibiotics |
| **Ebola, Hemorrha-gic Fevers** | Viruses | Fever, vomiting, diarrhea, sore throat, generalized pain or malaise, internal & external bleeding | Supportive, antiviral |
| **Plague (Bubonic, Septicemic, Pneumonic)** | Bacteria in flea bite | Swollen glands, lumps in axillas & groin, pneumonia, bloody emesis, joint pain | Antibiotics |
| **SARS (Severe acute respiratory syndrome)** | Rotavirus | Fever, myalgia, lethargy, gastrointestinal symptoms, cough, sore throat, shortness of breath | Steroids, riboviran, supportive |

# HIV/AIDS

This chapter would not be complete without some mention of HIV/AIDS. Medical professionals have access to a great deal of information about this disease, from the earliest recognition in 1981 to the present cocktail of treatments. We know the clinical picture of HIV/AIDS. We understand the devastation of the diagnosis to the person, the family and society. Now, disease is changing the social and economic structure of the entire continent of Africa as it affects the wage-earning generation, leaving orphans to fend for themselves.

HIV/AIDS knows no boundaries, affecting newborns and adults, men and women, homosexual and heterosexual, those who use illicit drugs and those who have never touched a needle. Like the Samaritan woman at the well, its victims often bear a social stigma and become outcasts. This disease emphasizes the link between body, mind and soul that medical care must address.

Persons infected with HIV/AIDS are children of God who need the Living Water. Their families, parents and children, as well as you and I line up together at the well ready to offer Christ a cup so that He might give us the water of eternal life.

> ... *Jesus, tired as he was from the journey, sat down by the well. It was about the sixth hour. When a Samaritan woman came to draw water, Jesus said to her, "Will you give me a drink?"*
> *(His disciples had gone into the town to buy food.)*
>
> *The Samaritan woman said to him, "You are a Jew and I am a Samaritan woman. How can you ask me for a drink?" (For Jews do not associate with Samaritans.)*
>
> *Jesus answered her, "If you knew the gift of God and who it is that asks you for a drink, you would have asked him and he would have given you living water."*

# Who Am I that I Should Go?

*"Sir," the woman said, "you have nothing to draw with*
*and the well is deep. Where can you get this living water?*
*Are you greater than our father Jacob, who gave us the*
*well and drank from it himself, as did also his sons*
*and his flocks and herds?"*

*Jesus answered, "Everyone who drinks this water*
*will be thirsty again, but whoever drinks the water I give*
*him will never thirst. Indeed, the water I give him will*
*become in him a spring of water welling up to*
*eternal life."*
John 4: 6-14

We can place no judgment on the poor, hungry, naked, jailed or sick, whom God has called us to serve. Like Moses, we only ask: "Who am I that I should go?"

## Action Plan

### Personal response:
Expect God to be an active member of your team.

### Awareness:
Become familiar with the prevalent illnesses in the area where you will be.

### Making a Difference:
Add prayer to your holistic care-giving practice.

\* \* \*

*On a medical team, lives are saved...*
*Souls are comforted, hearts are opened,*
*Hope if offered, love is shared, faith is built.*

# Who Am I that I Should Go?

## About the Author

Joyce Good Henderson has been active in local, national and international missions for more than thirty years. She has led eleven teams on short-term missions to Ecuador in the past nine years. She serves as the head of the Missions Board at her church, CenterPointe Church of Palm Bay, FL.

In addition to her work in Ecuador, she has participated and led many one-day projects in her community, in neighboring counties and state. She has developed curriculum for team leaders and members in cross-cultural missions, and participated in and taught training workshops.

A nurse for more than forty years, Joyce Good Henderson is a community-based homecare nurse, writer and photographer. Her book publication credits include: *Starting a Successful Writing Business*; *Before You Call Mom: A Real Life Survival Guide*; *So You Have to Do a Science Fair Project*; *Strategies for Winning Science Fair Projects*; *Children of the Kingdom*; and *A Special Kind of Parenting.*

She works with several mission organizations and sponsors children through Compassion International and World Vision.

While there are hundreds of wonderful mission sending organizations, she recommends:

Servants in Faith and Technology
2944 County Road 113 - Lineville AL 36266
www.sifat.org

\* \* \*

Oaks Of Righteousness
436 Aruba Ct.
Satellite Beach, FL 32937

www.ingramcontent.com/pod-product-compliance
Lightning Source LLC
La Vergne TN
LVHW051458080426
835509LV00017B/1798